# WHAT TO DO
# AFTER
# YOU TURN OFF
# THE TV

# WHAT TO DO
# AFTER
# YOU TURN OFF
# THE TV

## Fresh Ideas for Enjoying Family Time

# Frances Moore Lappé and Family

## Illustrated by Kevin Bartlett and Anthony Lappé

**Ballantine Books · New York**

Library of Congress Catalog Card Number: 85-90572
ISBN: 0-345-31660-6

Cover design by Georgia Morrissey

*Manufactured in the United States of America*

First Edition: October 1985

10   9   8   7   6   5   4   3   2   1

*To Ina Moore, my mother,*
*whose generous and courageous*
*spirit lights our lives*

# Contents

# Acknowledgments

This book is truly a cooperative effort of family, friends and strangers
. . . and strangers who became friends in the course of writing it.

First, we want to thank Rhea Irvine for her tireless effort and creative suggestions. Her inspired assistance made the book possible.

Nancy DeSalvo, librarian in Farmington, Connecticut, also has our gratitude. She generously offered her time and contacts in acquainting us with her town's "TV Turn Off." Our friend Jerry Mander inspired us with his groundbreaking *Four Arguments for the Elimination of Television* and contributed critical insights for this book.

We also want to offer special thanks to the many contributors you will find throughout the book who were willing to share glimpses of their family life with us. Their experiences and insights add enormously to our book: Mary Allan, Mary Anderson, Bill Ayers, Joshua Banner, Gigi Barth, Deya Brashears, Kristine Brown, Kira Brunner, Kevin Cadogan, Pat Cody, Isa Cohen, Sandra Cohn, Suzanne Copeland, Janaki Costello, Debbie Coyle, Debbie Devney, Leah Potts Fisher, Matthew Gaines, the Galarza Family, Meadow Goddard, Gretta Goldenman, Doug and Karen Goodkin, Sandy Goralnick, Mark Gordon, Tim Gordon, Leila Graves, Gwen Green, Joan and Alan Gussow, Tamiko Harris, Betty Henry, Doris Hill, Evan Hopewell, Miriam Hutchins, Sisse Jensen, Valerie and Larry Jordon, Forest Kan, Mark Kannett, Kathy Kolman, Sally and Gordon Lake, Clyde Leland, Elaine Magree, Donna Mickleson, Fred Mindlin, Tom and Lindsay Mugglestcue, Margo Nanny, Eugene Nelson, Janice Newton, Gene Novak, Arrow Thompson Olesky, Kate Olsen, Alexis Parks, Andrea Persky, Sulamith Potter, Julian Prindle, Linda Ream, Leonard Rifas, Amelia Ross-Gibson, Benji and Nathaniel Rudiak-Gould, Nancy Schimmel, Kathy and Anna Severens, Colleen and Milo Shannon-Thornberry, Donna Shultz, Kayla Starr, Molly Sullivan, Julie Summers, David Thompson, Jim Thurston, Lisa Van

Dusen, Gabriel Wachob, Craig White, Claire Wickens, Sheila and Brook Wilensky-Lanford, Suzanne Williams, Linda and Jim Young and Tom Zink.

Finally, we wish to thank Joan Raines, our literary agent, for her enthusiastic support for this project from its inception and Joëlle Delbourgo of Ballantine Books for her careful attention and creativity in making our book attractive and inviting.

# WHAT TO DO
# AFTER
# YOU TURN OFF
# THE TV

# 1
# Is There Life After TV?

**A** salesperson for cable TV came to our door a few years ago. When I told him I wasn't interested because I didn't own a TV, his eyes widened: "My God," he said, "you're like the buffalo!"

Well, maybe he was right—families like mine may be close to extinction. Even we bought a set the next year. Maybe the buffalo won't return to the prairie—after all, the average TV-viewing time in American households is up to 7.2 hours a day and still climbing.

Yet despite such staggering statistics, we're convinced that the great American love affair with television has begun to fizzle. And, it's not just because so many of the shows are lousy. More and more Americans are beginning to feel uneasy about the medium itself—about the dominant role it plays in our lives. In fact, you probably would not have picked up this book had you not shared this uneasiness.

So, why don't more of us just turn it off—or toss it out altogether?

Our hunch is that a lot of people fear that when they open the closet door to stash away the TV, out will pop another monster—that great Fear of the Void. I know that fear well, that sinking "what will we DO all weekend? The kids will drive me crazy!" feeling. Yes, I've faced that monster and lived to tell about it. We all can. But some ideas from those who have themselves leaped into that void will help. And that is what this book is about.

We've chosen to make at least half of our book activities that families can do together. We want to explain why.

## WHAT IS "FAMILY"?

There's a lot of talk about "family" these days, a lot of hand wringing over its demise. But even those most distressed about threats to the family have few ideas about how to strengthen it. Some cling to the form, wishing that somehow we could promote marriage or encourage parents to enforce rules better in the home.

But families aren't marriages or homes or rules. Families are people who develop intimacy because they live together, because they share experiences that come over the years to make up their uniqueness— the mundane, even silly traditions that emerge in a group of people who know one another in every mood and circumstance. It is this intimacy that provides the grounding for our lives.

TV robs us of these family-building traditions. One, it's passive. TV doesn't allow us to show one another who we are; so how could it be a vehicle for us to get to know one another? Two, we're all watching the same shows. So even if we do sit and watch together, how can we come to feel our own family's specialness? It's only when we turn off the TV that we can make that discovery.

## "DOWNTIME"—THE BENEFITS OF BOREDOM?

Most of us would admit that we often turn on the TV not to see a particular program, but simply to escape boredom. It's taken for granted—for who likes being bored?

When I began working on this book, I got in touch with an old friend, Jerry Mander, who wrote a book, *Four Arguments for the Elimination of Television*,[1] that I had been recommending for years. I discovered that Jerry is completing another, more comprehensive book on the impact of technology to be published by Sierra Club Books. In it, he introduces the concept of "downtime"—an intriguing notion that is central to the challenge of *What to Do After You Turn Off the TV*. I can do no better than to quote Jerry:

---

1. Jerry Mander, *Four Arguments for the Elimination of Television* (New York: Morrow Quill Paperbacks, 1978).

I am a member of the pre-TV generation. Until I was 14 or 15 we had no television. And I can still remember what it felt like to come home every day. First, I'd go look in the kitchen or refrigerator to see if there were any special snacks my mother left for me. I'd take care of those. Then, slowly becoming bored, I'd play with the dog for a bit. Here comes the boredom. Nothing to do.

Slowly, I'd slip into a kind of boredom that seemed awful. An anxiety went with it, and a gnawing tension in the stomach. It was exceedingly unpleasant, so unpleasant that I would eventually decide to act—to *do* something. I'd call a friend, I'd go outdoors. I'd go play ball. I'd read. I would do something.

Looking back, I view that time of boredom, of "nothing to do," as the pit out of which creative action springs. Taking all young people together, you could think of it as a kind of genetic pool of creativity. You got to the bottom of your feelings, you let things slip to their lowest ebb, and *then* you take charge of your life. Not wanting to stay in that place, you make an act. You experience yourself in movement, with ideas, in action.

Nowadays, however, at the onset of that uncomfortable feeling, kids usually reach for the TV switch. TV blots out both the anxiety and the creativity that might follow.

Jerry's words hit home. None of us wants to admit that anxiety could have a positive role in our lives. We just want to get rid of it! Forever, if possible. And we use the TV to help us.

But ultimately our strategy is self-defeating. The greatest anxiety that most of us experience is the anxiety of not knowing who we are or where we're headed. TV may help us avoid the daily anxiety of deciding how to use our leisure, only to trap us into the worst anxiety of all—a fear that we've never discovered who we are.

## SELF-DISCOVERY

Although we were the last family on our block to get a TV, I watched my share. Sitting through my youth in front of TV and in traditional classrooms, I was a "success" academically and socially, by all external measures. Yet I reached my mid-twenties feeling vacant, totally unsure whether I had interests that were genuinely mine.

Only when I forced myself to let go of traditional learning structures and created a big (terrifying) void did I begin to discover interests of my own. Before too long my interests led to the pursuit of the political and economic roots of world hunger, leading me to write *Diet for a Small Planet*[2] in 1969 and co-founding the Institute for Food and Development Policy six years later. My life was transformed.

My point is that none of us need grow up feeling empty, unsure of our own unique personalities. We can come to appreciate—and release—the interests, tastes, curiosities inside to guide us from our earliest years. But this discovery cannot happen if we are merely sitting in front of a television. Of this I am convinced.

Writ even larger, we see all around us the evil wrought by passivity, by people being so unsure of their own values that they are easily swayed by others. And the inhumanity that flows from psychological underdevelopment is all too evident—people's readiness to put down a neighbor of a different color or class because they themselves have so little self-respect. Beginning to unplug ourselves from TV-learned passivity that robs us of self-knowledge, and therefore self-respect, will not solve our nation's problems, of course. But we're convinced that taking this initiative is not only a step in discovering ourselves but in building a true democracy of people who are able to think for themselves.

## WHAT TV TEACHES

While our special concern about America's TV culture is what it precludes rather than its active harm, we cannot overlook the mounting evidence that TV is an actual impediment to development.

First, there's the medium itself. By its very nature it teaches us to

2. Frances Moore Lappé, *Diet for a Small Planet*, 10th anniversary ed. (New York: Ballantine Books, 1982).

be passive: Entertainment, and even learning, becomes something we effortlessly receive, not our active creation. By its format—complex drama reduced to twenty-two-minute segments—TV teaches that even the most difficult life crises can be divided up into neatly solvable problems. How, then, do we acquire the tolerance for ambiguity and the perseverance needed in meeting real-life problems?

Within those twenty-two-minute segments, television is chopped up into tiny bite-sized pieces, each marked by change of sound or color or perspective to capture our attention. TV thus builds attention spans of only a few minutes' duration.

The significance of this aspect of TV's impact became real to me this year when I visited Farmington, Connecticut, a suburb of Hartford. Farmington had just gained international attention for its "TV Turn Off," in which more than a thousand Farmington residents pledged not to turn on the tube for a whole month. (You'll hear more about Farmington's experiment in our final chapter.)

I talked with Nancy DeSalvo, Farmington's librarian and chief instigator of the "TV Turn Off." As a librarian, she'd been well positioned to monitor TV's impact on children, she told me. To make her point, she brought out two books. One was a beautiful Lapp fairytale with dramatic and intricate illustrations. It had about forty to sixty words on each page. "This is the type of book I read to first-graders about ten years ago. It held their attention. They loved it." Then she opened the second book. It was a "pop-up" book—the kind in which the illustrations literally pop off the page. The illustrations were "cute," with little detail. It had about ten to twenty words to the page. "Today, in reading to first-graders, this is the only kind of book that will hold their attention." Mrs. DeSalvo is convinced that TV has been responsible for this dramatic decline. "If the book requires imagination or real concentration, they get very restless," she said.

The Lapp fairy tale versus the pop-up book summed up for me one dimension of what academic accounts describe as TV's role in "diminished attention spans," "language-development difficulties," or the "stunting of imagination."

But there is another dimension to TV's impact that had also been somewhat abstract to me until I visited Farmington. It has to do with the violent content of TV's programming.

Janice Newton is a Farmington kindergarten teacher whose experience convinces her that TV violence directly contributes to the aggressive behavior of children. "'The A Team' is my students' favorite show," she told me. "Normally on Wednesdays, the morning after 'The A Team,' their play is more violent. They tend to mirror what they see on TV." During Farmington's "TV Turn Off," she noticed less pushing and shoving on the playground. (We should add here that "The A-Team," with thirty-nine violent acts per hour, was ranked as television's most violent program in 1983.[3])

Do Janice Newton's personal observations find support among behavorial scientists? We turned to the literature on television's impact to find out.

What is the link between watching violence on TV and violent behavior? *Is* there a link? If you, like us, have not followed the issue closely, you too may have gotten the impression that there is considerable debate among scientists about the answer to these questions. The impression of debate arises, we learned, primarily from the 1972 Surgeon General's report on television and social behavior. The first press coverage of the report's conclusions exonerated television: TV VIOLENCE HELD UNHARMFUL TO YOUTH read *The New York Times* headline. Many of the scientists contributing to the report immediately protested that their research findings had been misrepresented.[4] But it was too late. In the public mind, the impression stuck that we have insufficient evidence to indict TV violence.

In their exhaustively researched book *The Early Window: Effects of Television on Children and Youth*, Robert M. Liebert and his coauthors suggest that this impression was misleading—and in large part due to the influence of the five members of the broadcasting industry

3. *San Francisco Chronicle*, March 18, 1983, quoting the National Coalition on Television Violence.
4. Robert M. Liebert, Joyce N. Sprafkin and Emily S. Davidson, *The Early Window: Effects of Television on Children and Youth*, 2nd ed. (New York: Pergamon Press, 1982), pp. 100 ff.

who served on the commission responsible for the report. To demonstrate how conclusive the evidence really is, they quote, for example, a statement by pediatrician Michael Rothenberg in the December 1975 issue of the *Journal of the American Medical Association:*

> One hundred forty-six articles in behavioral science journals, representing 50 studies involving 10,000 children and adolescents from every conceivable background, all showed that violence viewing produces increased aggressive behavior in the young. . . .[5]

If the topic weren't so deadly serious, Rothenberg's summary could make one chuckle. It took fifty scientific studies to show what—if you just think about it for a moment—is all too obvious. If, by demonstrating its supposed effects, television can make us go out and buy a new shampoo, why wouldn't it, of course, be able to convince us to use violence—just by showing how terrifically effective it can be?

In 1982, the U.S. Department of Health and Human Services released a report reviewing ten years of research. It concluded that "the effects of televised violence may be even more extensive than suggested by earlier studies. . . ."[6] The evidence is clearly in.

Precisely because of this commonsense (as well as the scientifically established) link between TV violence and aggression, for at least twenty years, parents, psychologists and educators have been raising worried, often angry voices against what they see as inordinate violence on television. During this same period, we've experienced our society becoming more and more violent and increasingly fearful. Yet, despite the general hue and cry and the conscientious efforts of organized public-interest groups, the level of TV violence has not decreased—if anything, it has gotten worse! Indeed, according to the National Coalition on Television Violence, in 1983 violence on prime-time network television reached its highest level since 1967—

5. Ibid., p. 105.
6. *Television and Behavior: Ten Years of Scientific Programs and Implications for the Eighties,* vol. 1, Summary Report, U.S. Dept. of Health and Human Services, Washington, D.C., 1982, p. 90.

there are *almost nine acts of violence during every hour of prime-time viewing.*[7] And violence in children's cartoons—twenty-one incidents per hour—is three times more frequent than in adult crime dramas.[8]

Not only is there evidence that television violence makes young people more aggressive, just as disturbing are signs that it may make us more fearful and less caring. One 1979 study of almost six hundred adolescents concluded that heavy television viewing was associated with a "heightened and unequal sense of danger and risk in a mean and selfish world."[9] Critics have pointed out that youth who watch a lot of TV might be those with more apprehensive personalities to begin with. Nevertheless, the findings are disturbing. Again, they confirm our commonsense judgment that the more violence we see on the screen, the more violence we can expect to find in the world.

Equally distressing are studies showing that by repeated exposure to violence on TV young children become less caring. Again, these studies came to life for me through the experience of the Farmington teacher, Janice Newton. She told me that in earlier years, whenever a child got hurt in the classroom or playground, others would gather around. It was a "big deal." The children showed concern and compassion for each other. Now that is changing, she said—and she's convinced that TV has played a role in the change. "Exposed to so much violence on TV, the children no longer show the empathy for one another that is so natural for five-year-olds."

## SO WHO WANTS IT?

Because we don't want to overload our introductory chapter with the negative, we won't go on about the many other criticisms we hear of TV programming—sex stereotyping, the underrepresentation of minorities, the concentration of junk food ads during children's viewing hours and so on. (The bibliography at the end of chapter eleven includes material concerned with these additional fail-

7. Op. cit., *San Francisco Chronicle.*
8. *TV and Growing Up*, New York City Board of Education, Office of Curriculum Development and Support, Publications Sales Office, Room 136, 110 Livingston Street, Brooklyn, N.Y. 11201, p. 40.
9. Op. cit., *The Early Window*, p. 126.

ings of television.) We will conclude this brief discussion by simply asking: With so much criticism of TV programming, why hasn't it gotten better?

Since you may share these criticisms and hear your friends complain about TV, you might wonder, like we do, why don't *our* opinions count? Part of the answer is that we don't all have equal votes when it comes to TV programming. The heavy viewers are decisive. And those who have given up on TV have no say at all. Although almost all households in America own at least one television, one-third of that potential audience does two-thirds of the viewing. And it's to these steady TV viewers that the networks gear their programming choices.[10]

Another reason that TV programming has not changed is that efforts to reduce TV violence have been consistently met with cries of protest against infringement of First Amendment rights of free speech. I have thought a great deal about this argument. Is it appropriate, I wonder, to place TV programming under the heading of "rights"? Might it not be best for our society to limit the concept of "rights" to those actions that are available to all, more or less equally? That is, the right to say what we please publicly and to write and distribute our own views. But access to television is available only to the tiny handful who can afford it. Their wealth allows them to bring their images into our homes. Might this access be more aptly termed a privilege—now granted by wealth—rather than a right? And, it would seem, any privilege carries with it responsibility.

Many other democracies—those in Scandinavia or Japan, for example—assume that society and the TV networks share a mutual responsibility to make sure that TV programming is not destructive, particularly to children.

## "IT TURNED OUT TO BE REAL EASY"

But the whole point of our book is not to frighten you away from TV but to entice you away! Many of us already see for ourselves the detriment that heavy TV viewing can be to developing rich family

10. Op. cit., *The Early Window*, p. 23.

lives. Few of us have to be told.

But then the question arises, Since TV *is* a very effective escape from boredom and hooks many of us like any other addiction, isn't turning it off a heavy challenge indeed? Won't we have months of "withdrawal" symptoms to cope with?

Surprisingly, what we've found is that many people discover turning off the TV to be easier than they had expected. Something we should never forget about children is that they learn *very fast*. This means they can pick up new habits more quickly than we might imagine.

As a case in point, Sandy Goralnick, who participated in Farmington's "TV Turn Off," related her experience with her three-year-old daughter. Her daughter had been quite sick a few months before, so Sandy had encouraged a lot of television watching to keep her quiet. Cartoons were the first thing she would ask for when she got up in the morning. "She watched every day," Sandy told me,

> So, when the "TV Turn Off" started, I was real nervous. She had become so addicted to the TV that I thought she'd fuss a lot and make life miserable. But I just explained to her that everyone was involved—the library and the schools, and she accepted it.
>
> And now she does not even think of TV. It's amazing what a month could do for a child that age. She just walks right by it and doesn't even think of turning it on. I am really shocked. I wouldn't have believed it.

With older children, readjustment and discovery may take longer . . . but not forever. Alexis Parks, a magazine publisher in New York City, tells of her experience of "doing away with the TV set":

> There was, perhaps, a month's worth of arguing. I listened to, responded to and ignored their pleas daily. . . . And then something magical happened:
>
> They adjusted. I used to tell a friend that from that time on, coming home to my kids was like coming home to the Waltons. They talked together, they did their homework, they played board games and even practiced their music, . . . uninterrupted

by the captive fascination of the TV screen. It was lovely.

Did they miss it? At first. But they soon discovered that "not having one" became a sign of distinction for them with their peers. They became more thoughtful. They liked being different.

Many participating in Farmington's experiment were surprised at how quickly their habits could change. A third-grader said, "Boy, there really are a lot of things to do without watching television. It was nice without it. At first I thought it would be really hard, but it turned out to be real easy."

We don't deny, however, that cutting down on TV viewing, or removing television from your lives, may cause some conflict initially. But it will ultimately reduce conflict. One of Alexis Parks's motives in getting rid of television was that she had become "tired of being a watchdog, nag . . . and tie breaker on the programs my children wanted to watch."

"Which show to watch" ranks among the top three sources of family disputes in America. One of our young contributors to this book told us about her family's Saturday morning arguments. "My brother and I wanted to watch cartoons. My father always wanted to watch 'Sesame Street,' seriously. We would get into these big arguments about what to watch. Every weekend."

Taking charge of our TV viewing will reduce this conflict.

## COLD TURKEY?

In this book, we are *not* advocating that we all get rid of our TVs! I mentioned that we did get a set ourselves. It sits in the closet waiting for a program so special that we feel like pulling it out.

It is true, however, that when my children were little, it was much easier not to have a TV at all than to haggle over the number of hours they could watch. Moving from New York to California in 1977 seemed like a good time to make some big changes—so I just gave my TV away. And the kids never protested. No TV was definitely the right answer for me then. But if you would not consider my cold-turkey approach, there are ways to reduce the hours in front of the tube without having a family debate each time the switch goes on or off.

In chapter eleven, we discuss a variety of approaches to regaining control over TV without getting rid of it altogether.

## WHY WE WROTE THIS BOOK

We've written our book for both kids and adults. Since I've worked full-time since Anna was two and a half, I know what it's like to come home exhausted and be tempted simply to turn on the TV to get the kids out of my hair. But, unfortunately, what starts out as occasional relief, too often becomes habitual. Sure, we feel guilty about using the TV as a baby-sitter, but without any conceivable alternative, how hard it is to change? We hope that our book challenges both kids and adults to look at even this stressed time differently—to see new possibilities. Turning off the TV need not mean a greater "burden" on parents: This book suggests that kids can become more self-reliant.

Not only was our book written for children, it was written *with* children. Anthony (age thirteen) and his cousin, Kevin Bartlett (age fifteen) have illustrated it. Anna (age ten) has contributed many ideas she's come up with to enjoy herself, by herself, or with her friends. Even though chapter nine, "Just Plain Fun," focuses on kids-only play, *in almost every chapter, you'll discover that more than half of the experiences we share need not involve adults at all.*

But we also hope that adults reading our book will find their assumptions about "baby-sitting" shaken up a bit. It is so easy to think of time with our kids as a drag, taking us away from our work or our own fun. But, if we can let go of preconceived notions, maybe more of the activities we do *with* our kids can relax and entertain us, too.

Let's be perfectly frank, though. If you really desire to use the TV baby-sitter less and to enjoy yourself with your children more but feel resentful and exhausted instead, maybe what you need first is not any of these ideas but a *break!* Such is the sage advice of Leah Potts Fisher, a psychotherapist and mother who contributed some neat ideas for this book. Leah wrote,

With my own children, I find that when I start feeling down on myself as an inattentive parent, when I start to run out of creative ideas or lack energy to implement the ideas I have, often what I need is a day all to myself, a chance to write in my journal, to make the lists and plans which give me a sense of control, a chance to go hiking alone and regain perspective. I usually return much happier with myself and my children and more able to be with them in playful ways.

My own version of Leah's philosophy is simply to remind myself constantly that I cannot rear happy children unless I am happy with my life. Part of this is looking inside myself before any activity to ask, "Do I really want to be doing this?" Where possible, I try to do only what I enjoy; when that's impossible, at least I'm not fooling myself!

## HOW WE WROTE THIS BOOK

The idea for this book came to me one nothing-special evening when the kids and I were hanging out in the living room, doing homework and reading. Looking at them, I realized that the "little kid" days were gone. I have been divorced since 1977, so the three of us have spent a good deal of time alone together. And since I share custody, no doubt my time with them has seemed even more precious to me. But more and more, I realized, their friends would become the center of their lives, not their parents. I was clutched with nostalgia for all our nothing-special times together, and some of our special times, too. I felt determined not to forget, nor even to take those years for granted.

So in addition to being a response to my deep concern about television's erosion of family life, this book became, very personally, my way of never forgetting. The kids and I had fun racking our brains to recall our antics of years past. Often they remembered details that I had completely lost. And I started paying more attention to how the kids use their time now.

Then we turned to others for help. We contacted friends whose family lives I knew to be especially rich. Several—the Gussows and the Severens, for example—were gold mines of ideas, as you will see. And we placed stories in community newspapers and an inexpensive ad in one national magazine asking people to share their experiences with us. Our assistant, Rhea Irvine, a gifted teacher, with many contacts with children, passed out dozens of questionnaires to both teachers and family friends. Some teachers used our questionnaire as a class writing assignment: "What Do You Do After You Turn Off the TV?"

All together, we received hundreds of responses and wove the best ones into our own experiences to build the book. Once we had a first draft, we circulated it to all contributors and invited those near us to an evening of getting to know one another and further brainstorming. As we hoped, this stimulated their memories anew—so still more ideas popped up.

One of the best rewards of this process is that the families you will meet in our book come in all varieties—big and small, two-parent and single-parent, mother working in the home and outside the home. Some have TVs; others do not. You will hear mothers', fathers', grandparents' and children's voices.

Our ultimate dream for this book is that it will become a living document—renewed and improved every few years by suggestions from our readers. So, please, as you read, jot down your family's experiences. Send them to us for inclusion in future editions. Remember, what seems ordinary to you may be a delightful novelty to someone else.

## NOT A GAME HOUSE, BUT A WAY OF LIVING

We have organized our book into themes, or types of activities, rather than by age (the exception being chapter four, which is for toddlers and young children)—for two reasons. First, many of the ideas can appeal to any age. Second, and most important, we want more to inspire than to instruct; we hope that the theme approach will stimulate you to think up your own variations, not feel you must repeat what someone else has done. Our purpose is not to tell you what to do—you'll come up with a pattern of less-TV (or TV-less) living unique to you.

We have also concentrated on activities that require little or no equipment, as well as on indoor, as opposed to outdoor, ideas, since it is often evening hours and rainy, cold days that seem hardest for kids to fill without television. To make it easier for you to find ideas appropriate to your family, we have coded each to indicate which are good for the whole family, which are suited for kids by themselves, and which are best for the very young.

 *The Whole Family*     *Kids by Themselves*     *Very Young Kids*

But in writing an activities book, we fear that we inadvertently make ourselves appear a little peripatetic, as if our home is a game house in which we're all rushing from one activity to the next! In reality, these activities have developed over many years. Remember, too, to expect some flops, some disappointments, as your family begins to develop new patterns. That's okay. It's part of learning to be one's own judge and not to accept prepackaged programs—even ours!

Finally, we realize that in focusing on specific activities we cannot capture the glue—the attitudes and the assumptions—that holds together our lives. But you'll discover it. You'll learn that what can emerge without the intrusion of television is the interlinking of our lives, so that the issue is not "What activity can I, the parent, dream up to entertain my children?" but rather, finding a way of living in which children and adults share not only satisfying leisure time but work and study time, too.

In this vein, then, our most precious moments are hardest to capture in a book. They are the quietest ones, those hardest to "sell." You'll no doubt discover more of those moments, too. Without the TV for people to rush to, maybe mealtime conversation will begin to lengthen and become more interesting. Maybe your family will discover the pleasure of just sitting together in the living room, listening to music or reading your favorite books.

Who knows what can happen once you face the GREAT VOID, full of delightful possibilities?

# 2

# Games for the Whole Family

## WORD AND STORY GAMES

### Geography—A Storytelling Game (by Ina Moore, Frances's Mother)

 Geography has to come first in our book. Our family's made its reputation on it! Now, please do *not* think that this game is only for those clever people who have a way with words. At age four, Anna played! I've seen adults who *swore* they couldn't do it get snuckered in . . . so beware.

We have watched Geography take over a holiday weekend of an extended-family gathering, causing each age group to forget to watch their favorite TV shows. We've seen it dominate family dinner parties. And don't be surprised if after playing for a while, one of your children greets you at the breakfast table with "I thought of a 'geography' when I went to bed last night. Want to hear it?"

The game is simple: Make up a story that ends with the name of a geographical location (state, country) left off for the listener(s) to guess.

It all started one day when Gil (Frances's brother) and Peter (Gil's son) were driving on a highway in Texas. Peter, noticing a Brownwood plate on the car ahead of them, asked, "Brown would what?" Gil pondered a moment before replying with the story that gave birth to this game:

Well, Brown had this son who dropped out of college, let his hair and beard grow long and straggly, and just stayed around the house strumming on a guitar. Eventually the worry and aggravation caused him to consider telling his son to shape up or ship out. But he couldn't bring himself to kick the kid out, because Mr. Brown would ? ? ? (See answer below.)

(You see, it's okay to take some poetic license with pronunciation! In fact, the liberties with pronunciation are a big part of the fun.)

Since that fated day, it has become a family tradition spreading through the various "branches" and among our friends. Geography has become almost an identifier of belonging to the clan, reminiscent of the "olden days" before radio and television, when family gatherings were rich with real-life stories passed down—and perhaps embellished through the years—from generation to generation.

A family playing Geography will develop its own repertoire of "classics" with which to introduce the game to the uninitiated. As with all games played with mixed age groups, you can vary the level of difficulty so that everybody can participate.

When Anna was still in preschool, Anthony (who is two years older) would team up with her for a turn. It wasn't long until she thought up one on her own, and her delight that Anthony "got it" launched her into storytelling. "Oregon!" Anthony shouted when he guessed the ending of her account of an old man adrift in a rowboat because . . . because his "oar gone!"

Don't make the mistake that any mixed-age-group game should all be played down to a child's level of comprehension. As long as opportunities are interspersed for their full participation, they will enjoy and learn from the antics of their elders. In this game, states and countries with which they are familiar can be used, with clues

(ANSWER: *Mississippi*, sounding like "miss his hippie.")

given such as "one of the United States" or "a country in western Europe."

The following are two of our family favorites, which can be told with embellishments of details and characterizations, according to the imagination of the storyteller. The first was Gil's and the second, Francie's (Frances's family nickname).

Sergeant Preston of the Northwest Mounted Police was summoned to London some years ago by Queen Elizabeth for the annual ceremony in which titles were conferred upon individuals for exceptional service to the Crown. As we all know, Sergeant Preston was devoted to his equally valiant dog, King, so he agreed to go only if King could accompany him. Thus it was that on the appointed day, attired in his handsome Mountie dress uniform, Preston approached the queen on her throne in Westminster Abbey with King at his side.

Now, it is not generally known that Queen Elizabeth is very nearsighted—and as vain about her appearance as any commoner. Thus she never wears her glasses when performing duties of state, depending on the lady-in-waiting who is always at her side to keep her apprised of what is going on.

So it was that when Sergeant Preston and King advanced down the aisle and knelt in front of her, the queen saw little more than a blur of figures. She raised her scepter and intoned the appropriate words, then lowered the sword all according to the age-old custom. But, hark, there arose in the abbey a quite unusual and unaccustomed titter. Confused and disturbed, the queen gestured for the ear of her lady-in-waiting and whispered, "What's wrong? What happened!" to which her attendant murmured (with some exasperation, since English commoners are devoted to protocol and correctness in their monarchs), " ? ? ? !"

Now, it's true, we'll admit, that not many people have ever guessed this one. The few who have guessed it have gone down in our "Geography hall of fame." But if the stories are good, it really doesn't matter if no one can guess the answer. The storyteller has so much fun stumping people!

Francie's story about a young couple during the time of the building of the pyramids in ancient Egypt is a little easier. Quite a few have guessed correctly. Can you?

Via and her young husband were always quarreling because he constantly complained

(ANSWER: *United Kingdom*, sounding like "You knighted King, Dumb!")

about how hard he had to work. Coming home
at night to their little lean-to in the conclave of
indentured workers near the pyramid site, he
would go on and on about the hot sun, the
blowing sand, the weight of the slabs of granite
he had to carry. And Via would go on and on
about how tired she was of listening to his
constant complaining.

One night he was especially irritable, and she
had had a hard time getting enough water to
prepare their supper, so she lashed back at him,
"It's no harder on you than the other men . . .
and in just a few years you will have earned our
freedom and we can go to Alexandria." He
moaned that he should live that long, and she
retorted that he had a strong physique and
should be able to do the work without his
continuous griping, to which he shouted back at

her, "Well, if you think it's so easy, then why
don't ? ? ? !" (See answer below.)

Don't be surprised if adults new to the game insist that they can't
come up with any stories. We've found that only a small percentage
fail eventually to burst out with "I've got one!"

And, once introduced to the fun of storytelling, children find that
the structure gives them ideas. At eleven, Anthony came up with a
dramatic tale about boxing, ending with ". . . it, Ali" (Italy) and one
about two roommates who just couldn't get along, ending with "Pack
it, Stan!" (Pakistan). When he was only nine, a riotous adventure—
which he explained took considerable poetic license with the name
of a country his mother was currently studying—ended with "Bong!
Go dash!" and, believe it or not, we were able to guess correctly—
Bangladesh.

The real fun is in the storytelling and listening to original tales.
Slick formula dramas on television quickly lose out in competition!
(As I write this, I just thought of one—it's about the Dallas Cowboy's
new jersey!)

The game has also inspired kids—and adults—to scour the globe
and the atlas for inspiration.

## Fictionary—Telling Truth from Fiction

 Actually, I had never known the name of this
game we'd played for years. In fact, I thought
we had made it up . . . until I got letters from
others recommending it. But just in case
you've never played, here's a peek at Fictionary.

We played as adults before the kids were born and then discovered
that kids, by the age of nine or ten, love it, too. The most recent
time we played Fictionary, Anna's friend Justine and Anthony's
friend Adam were spending the evening with us.

(ANSWER: *Yugoslavia*, pronounced, "you go slave, Via!")

Anthony was the dictionary keeper on our first round. He searched the dictionary and found a word that none of us knew the meaning of. "B-U-T-E-O," he spelled out for us to write down on slips of paper. (If anyone had known the word, he or she would have been obliged to say so, and Anthony would have had to find another.)

We each made up a definition and wrote it on our little piece of paper, trying to write in "dictionary-ese" in order to fool the others. While we invented definitions, Anthony wrote the real one on a slip of paper just like ours. He simplified it slightly so that it would sound more like one of us could have come up with it.

Here's what we wrote:

1. *Buteo:* the ceremonial sash worn by
      bullfighters in Spain
2. *Buteo:* a type of hawk with broad rounded
      wings and soaring flight
3. *Buteo:* a clay cup common in West Africa
4. *Buteo:* a device used by tailors to aid in
      sewing a straight seam
5. *Buteo:* a small mammal of the Australian
      outback

When finished, we all handed our definitions—folded so that no one could see—to Anthony. Anthony's job was to read all the definitions with a straight face, as if each were the real one. After all were read, we took turns guessing which was the real definition. The person to guess correctly gets to be the dictionary keeper. If more than one person guesses correctly, you can flip a coin for who goes first. (Would *you* have guessed correctly? Number 2.)

A fun twist on this game is to also ask each person to guess which definition was made up by which player. Trying to "psyche out" the others can be even more fun than guessing the correct definition.

(Remember, in this game it doesn't matter if the children don't know how to spell all the words in their definition. All that matters is that the dictionary keeper can read it. It's the dictionary keeper's job to read it so smoothly that it sounds official.)

## WORD GAMES WITH YOUNG CHILDREN

Although chapter four focuses exclusively on enjoying time with toddlers and preschoolers, I've included some simple games here that most children would enjoy once they are verbal.

### Add-On Stories

 When Anthony and Anna were smaller, Add-On Stories could make mealtime very special. It's so simple: Anyone starts a story and the person next to him/her continues it. Sometimes the tales get wild. Anyone can draw the story to a close, but it must really *end*.

Mark Gordon offered an interesting twist:

> Sometimes we add a "pointer" to our Add-On Story game. The pointer "conducts" the story, deciding who goes next and when. She can cut the speaker off, even in the middle of a sentence. The only rule we have is that there can be no non sequiturs in the story, no "The car was going ninety miles an hour—Please pass the salt!"

### Rhyming Hills

  When Anna asked her fourth-grade classmates what they like to do when they "turn off the TV," Doris Hill offered this rhyming word game:

> Ingredients: Your family or even you and your friends. A sense of voice. (You don't have to be really smart, but you can't be dumb.) Dice.
>
> Directions: Gather around in a circle. Now take the dice and take turns rolling it. The person with the highest number goes first. After that, just keep going counterclockwise. Now the first person shouts out a word and the next

person rhymes it. This keeps on going until
someone cannot rhyme it. If this happens, start
all over again. If you make it all around the
circle without somebody messing up, the person
next to the person counterclockwise who went
first the last time goes first. Do this over and
over again until your family or friend is bored.

## Mime Rhyme

  Here's an idea from Tom Zink that combines
rhyme and mime. It's simple: "You just say,
'I'm thinking of a word that rhymes with, for
instance, *air*,' and other players make their
guesses using gestures and movements without talking." Reading
this, Anna and I could already imagine ourselves guessing, by pretending to *tear* a piece of paper or prancing like a *mare*.

Tom suggests a good book for more ideas like this one: *Mime: A
Playbook of Silent Fantasy* by Kay Hamblin (New York: Doubleday,
1978).

## Action Adverb

  Sometimes even TV can be a source of ideas
for things families can do after it's turned off.
Sisse Jensen said that the TV movie that provided the source for this game was lousy, but
"we've had a lot of fun with the game."

Any age can join in. One of you goes out of the
room, and the others choose an adverb—*fast,
angrily, quickly, sleepily*. Then, the "guesser"
comes back in and asks one of the "insiders" to

do something in the way of the word. If the word is *quick*, for example, you'd see the person scurrying around. The "outsider" gets only five guesses to guess what the adverb is.

## GUESSING GAMES—NEW TWISTS

### Abstraction

 We learned this game as teenagers and then introduced it to Anna and Anthony when they were eight and eleven. In one of our most memorable games of abstraction, Anna was "it." She thought of a person (it had to be someone that everyone playing knows), and the rest of us had to guess who she had in mind by asking only such questions as "If he or she were a flower, what kind of flower would he or she be?" "If he or she were a car, what kind of car?" "If he or she were a color . . . ?" "an animal?" "a smell?" And on and on. The first person to guess who Anna was thinking of would win.

As Anna was answering the questions, I began to think that she had my mother in mind. When she was asked "What food?" for example, Anna answered, "Doughnuts"—and, well, my mom is notorious in our family for her sweet tooth. But then, we asked, "What animal?" When Anna answered, "Crab," I was a little taken aback. I knew she didn't think of her grandmother as crabby—so what could this mean? But Anthony guessed Gramma, and he was right.

"But, Anna, why on earth did you say, 'Crab'?" I asked. "Well," Anna explained, "aren't crabs kinds of animals that can grow back an arm or leg if they get one broken off? Gramma has had so many sicknesses in her life, and she hasn't let it stop her. She keeps going. That's why I thought of a crab."

I was amazed. She had gotten her biology wrong, but I didn't bother to make a point of that. She had beautifully expressed an insight into her grandmother that I had no idea she had. Games can be vehicles for many kinds of discoveries about your family.

### Charades—Variations on an Old Favorite

 Charades is great for "hams," which seem to be our family's strong suit. But we've discovered a variation of Charades especially for those who feel awkward standing up and looking foolish. It's team charades. Two people together act out the title (movie, play, book, or whatever). Especially for kids, teamwork makes it all much more fun. The pressure is off the individual to perform, and kids have fun combining forces to act out the words.

I suppose because games like Charades force us to let go of inhibitions, they generate some moments that go down in family history, moments that we delight in reliving years, even decades, later.

In our family, the great Charades never-to-be-forgotten "moment" occurred one evening about ten years ago during a family reunion in Texas (Gil and I were grown), when Mom succeeded in getting across a movie title in—well—not more than a full second.

Starting from the middle of the room, she simply backed out the doorway in a great *whoosh* that Tim and Anthony have illustrated for you.

Wouldn't *you* have yelled "Gone with the Wind"!?

## Newlyweds—Or, Do You *Really* Know Me?

 I'm sure you've seen or heard of the TV game show in which contestants have to answer questions requiring intimate knowledge of their loved ones. Well, we made up our version one night after the movies when we were lingering over ice cream in a local restaurant.

Four of us played: Anna and her buddy Justine Moore were one team, and our close friend Peter Barnes and I were the other. First Peter thought of a question for Justine. "What is the nicest compliment you could imagine receiving?" Justine then whispered her answer—"that I am a good ballet dancer"—to me. Now it was up to Anna to guess what Justine's answer was.

Sometimes the game can be a little disturbing, when someone you're close to doesn't know something about you that *you* think is basic! (Doesn't Peter know my favorite city in the world is *Rome*, not Paris!?) But it's also a means of getting to know each other. Some of Anna's answers were revealing.

The questions that people came up with that night included things like: "If you could choose one other city to live in besides this one, where would you live?" "What do you most like to do right before going to bed?" "What's your favorite dessert?" "Who do you think is the most easy-to-get-along-with person in your class?"

## Birthday Predictions

Several years ago we came up with this birthday ritual. Each of us, children and adults, on our birthday had to look—figuratively—into the crystal ball and guess what the future would bring.

We developed a list of questions to answer in writing. One for the kids. It included such questions as: What is your favorite sport at that time? your favorite activity? your favorite subject? your best friend? Another for the adults. Among the questions were: What is your major work project? Where will you be traveling? What will be your major concern? (Since we're all worriers!)

Then we put our answers in sealed envelopes in a special birthday-predictions box. We were not allowed to read our answers until the next birthday.

Opening the birthday predictions becomes another thing to look forward to on one's birthday. One of the side effects of our little ritual is to make us more aware of the patterns in our lives.

Rhea Irvine, our assistant on this book, has used another version with her fourth-grade classes. At the end of the calendar year, as one of the last activities before the Christmas holidays, the kids make New Year's predictions—what will happen next year? Families might have fun doing the same.

## GAMES OF THE SENSES—TOUCH, TASTE, SOUND

### Whose Ear Is This?

We take turns blindfolding each other and trying to identify each other by just touching one feature—the nose, a little finger, an ear, or whatever.

### Whose Voice Do You Hear?

Mark Gordon and his ten-year-old daughter, Cassie, made up a voice version of the previous game.

The listener sits with her back turned to the
other kids—blindfolded if you want. The
"chooser" silently points to one child, who
approaches the "it" talking in a disguised voice.
The listener can say, "Talk more," if she needs
to hear more. The only rule for the talker is that
she can't repeat anything that's been said before.
Some ways we've learned to disguise our voices:
Talk high or low. Use a foreign accent. Puff
your lips out or purse them very tight. And use
words that you don't usually use. Don't just say,
"Hi!"

## Taste Buds

  When Anna asked friends in her fourth-grade
class what they like to do when they turn off
the TV, Kira Brunner offered this:

All you need is a blindfold and lots of food.
Have someone put the blindfold on you and put
a lot of different kinds of food in different
bowls. Then take a food and eat it and try to
guess what it is. If you guess wrong, have them
put a black strip of paper in the bowl. If you
guess right, put a white strip in the bowl. Then
count how many you got right and wrong. If
you have more right than wrong, you have a
good sense of taste.

## Oregano or Rosemary, Please?

  Our sense of smell can also become a game
for little kids. The fun is in trying to see how
many herbs we can identify with our eyes
closed.

## What's Different?

I remember playing this in my front yard as a kid. When Anthony and Anna were much younger, I taught it to them. It's great when you don't have much energy but you want to spend time together. It teaches us to be observant:

Anthony's "it." He stands in front of us, and we examine him, tip to toe, front and back. Then, we turn our heads and close our eyes and count to twenty-five. While we're forbidden to look, he changes just *one* thing on his person, trying to make the least change possible. This time, he lifted a shirt label inside his back collar so it just barely peaked out from his shirt. We opened our eyes and had to start guessing what he had done. We never got it!

One thing about this game is that it gives messy dressers an advantage! It is also fun to add a few items of clothing or jewelry ahead of time so that you have more changes with which to baffle your family.

## ON-THE-ROAD GAMES

One of the pleasures of traveling is letting one's mind wander. Another can be that because you're all "trapped" together, exchanges occur that would never have happened at home.

Of course, there are old standard car pastimes—Ghost, and the kind of Geography that requires each person to think of a place name beginning with the final letter of the last person's contribution.

But what about making up your own free-association games?

### Naming Game

"On our way back from Mendocino," says Sulamith Potter, "we came up with one of our best word punning games. To play, you had to invent a personal name for an animal that incorporated its common biological name."

First we named the shells we'd found. One clam
was named Clamity Jane and another, Oh, My
Darling Clamentine. The abalone became Tai
Abalonia, after Tai Babilonia, the Olympic pairs
skating medalist. A hawk flying overhead
received the name Wild Bill Hick-hawk!

It was exciting . . . and we still add to it every
so often.

### License-Plate License

Making up people's names: "When I drive on
trips with my grandparents in West Virginia,"
eleven-year-old Evan Hopewell told me, "we
play a game they taught us. You see the first
letters on a license plate and make up a name. AB??? Albert
Bernstein."

A variation with older kids might be to limit names to those of
real people everyone in the car knows.

In our family, we've played an even looser version. We allow the
letters to suggest a word. Instead of looking at the individual letters
as initials, we look at the configuration of letters—JGM might become *judgment*. ONM might become . . . ? (One—literate—proof-
reader's answer was *onomatopoeia*!)

Then, there's always the fun of seeing who can count the most
out-of-state license plates.

### From "Alpine Road" to "Zenith Electric"

If you've ever wondered whether the next
town would have a pizza parlor (even though
you hate pizza) or ever searched the landscape
desperately for a Quik Stop, then you've
played this one.

It's so simple that any child can play it as soon as he or she knows
the alphabet. The game is a contest. Each person in the car tries to
locate in *alphabetical order* each letter of the alphabet on signs along

the road. When one person calls out the letter in a particular sign, no one else can use it. So you have to be quick, and, unfortunately, this sometimes means *loud*, as we get excited upon the discovery of such rarities as *q*'s and *z*'s.

We play two versions, depending on how long and hard we want to play. In our hard version, we can only use letters from official road signs. Now that means that finding a *z* can take some time, unless you happen to live near Zenith Road. Our easy version allows you to use commercial signs on stores and billboards.

Another A to Z game for young children comes from Betty Henry:

> The game starts with the sentence "My mother went on a trip and she brought . . ." Then the kids think of objects in alphabetical order. After the game, the children can draw pictures of poor Mom going on a trip with her alligator, button, crayons and so forth.

### Incongruous Images

 One of the themes of this book (if you haven't gotten it already!) is that being with our children can release the child in us, to our great pleasure. In part, this means learning that just being silly can be one of the greatest pleasures of all. We learn that the games we make up don't have to "make sense," have a point or carry a built-in lesson.

Betty Henry recalls how much fun it can be with little kids (her two- and seven-year-olds) to use the "mind wandering" pleasure of driving to come up with odd combinations, the wilder the better.

> It can be done at home, too, but the constantly changing scenery helps stimulate the imagination. What about a camel sitting on a telephone wire sipping tea? With the older children, we've pretended to be inventing new "California cuisine." Why not fish with chocolate sauce and cilantro?

*"What about a camel on a telephone wire sipping tea?"*

## Higgly Piggly

  Here's an "oldie" that we'd never played until recently, when Anna and I ended up on a nine-hour car trip observing farmworkers' conditions in Ohio and Michigan, as part of my work.

First you think up a rhyming adjective-noun combination—like "fat cat." Then you give the guessers a short definition—"Overweight feline?" Everyone has to guess the word combination. We didn't know the other three people in the car, but the game really broke the ice. One of our car companions was twelve years old and bilingual. So we tried to play in Spanish, too. But given my meager grasp of Spanish, all I could come up with was "a corn-cheese snack for he-men." Everyone got it—"Macho Nacho!"

To help the guessers, you indicate how many syllables are in your rhyming words by saying it's a "hig-pig," or a "higgly-piggly," or a "higgily piggily."

(Whoops, I just read in *Parlor Games*—recommended at the end of this chapter—that the real name of this game is Hink Pink. Oh well, if we can invent our own games, why not our own names?)

### Silly Names

  Here's a favorite from Lindsay Mugglestone, who you'll hear more from in the next chapter. She and her playmates thought they had made it up:

It's simple. You just try to come up with names that capture what the person does. Examples tell it all:

    Justin Case—insurance salesperson
    Susan Sox—footware salesperson
    Otto Rex—demolition driver
    Otto Lemmon—used-car dealer
You get the idea. The possibilities are endless!

### Travel Bingo

 We can't claim to have tried it, but the idea sounds like fun. Just make up your own bingo cards, using images that you are likely to see along the road: a water tower, a cow, a common fast-food chain, a car with a license plate from a noncontiguous state. Take the cards and pencils on the drive and check off those things you see. (Making up the cards could be as much fun as playing.) Just as in regular bingo, you win if you are the first to fill in a straight or diagonal line of images.

In another, simpler version, kids can make up color-dot bingo cards. The driver calls out colors ("A yellow truck!" "A blue house!"), and the players mark their cards. You can keep going until everyone has "won." This last idea came from *The Mother Earth News Almanac of Family Play* (see resource list in chapter three). It suggests using rimmed cookie sheets for instant "desks" on long car trips.

### Young Navigators

 I loved this suggestion from Sally and Gordon Lake, parents of twin four-year-olds:

On very short and familiar car trips (for example, to the grocery store), we ask our kids to pretend that we don't know how to get there. Our children have to tell *us* when and where to turn. If the turn is not announced, the driver just keeps going straight. Our children are thrilled to see that they are really navigating the car!

## AT-HOME GAMES

### Spoons

 Molly Sullivan's family offered one of their favorites for our book:

You need three or more players and a dealer; a
deck of cards; and a spoon for each of the
players minus one, just as in Musical Chairs.

Put the spoons in the center of the table, not
touching each other. Deal each person four
cards. The dealer then sits with the cards in a
stack facedown in front of him or her. The
dealer looks at the top card and passes it to the
first player, facedown. If this player doesn't want
the card, she passes it on to the next player. If
he wants it, he adds it to his hand and then
passes another card from his hand to the next
player. The dealer moves rapidly.

The aim is to get all four of the same number
card—all the aces, all the fours and so on. When
you do, you sneak a spoon from the center of
the table. If you see one person take a spoon,
you grab one yourself as fast as you can. The
person who ends up without the spoon gets an
S. The second time that person ends up without
a spoon, she gets a P and so on. The loser is the
first one to get S-P-O-O-N-S.

You end up either watching the spoons or
watching the cards. Lots of silly fun.

The Wickens family used to play Spoons on their camping trips during the long, dark hours before bed. "All of us lay in our sleeping
bags outdoors, positioned in a star formation with the spoons in the
center," recalls Claire.

## Doodle Games

Anna and her friends like to make up doodles (drawn
from unusual perspectives) and then have others guess
what they are. We have included two here that stumped
me.

a.)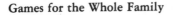

b.)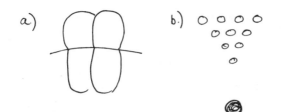

(Turn upside down for answers.)

B.  You're looking down at a bowling ball and pins.

A.  You're looking up at a man on a tightrope.

## Poker—From a Kid's Point of View

 We've gone through Poker phases. In the early years before we had the kids, we used to play Poker with our foreign coin collection—a tin box of coins of different shapes and metals from all over the world. We had fun dividing them up by size and settling on how much they were worth. We've also played with black beans and garbanzos from the kitchen.

One of my favorite versions of Poker we called Forehead. I am sure it's not original with us. We played regular Five-Card Draw, with the sole difference being that one card in your hand was held to the forehead so that everyone else could see it, but *you* could not. You had to guess what the fifth card in your hand might be, based on the expressions on the faces of the other players. I loved it, as I tried to keep a poker face myself while looking at other people's cards and trying to see through the poker faces of the others.

Especially since Anna had been the big winner the last time we played, I was intrigued by thirteen-year-old Gigi Barth's insight:

> When our family does something together, we
> play Poker. We don't use real money, just chips.
> Most of the time I win because my parents don't
> like to take the chances I do. Poker is really a

relaxing game. It's good to learn how far to go
with what risks.

## CAN HOLIDAYS REALLY BE FUN?

Holidays and other special occasions offer a lot of possibilities for
enjoying people we love. Unfortunately, for many of us—myself
included, more often than I'd like to admit—holidays feel like just
another burden. I've always wished I'd been better at devising our
own special holiday traditions. In chapter ten, we tell about families
adapting traditional holiday ceremonies to communicate values in a
way that they feel relevant to our children today. But here are some
more frivolous ideas:

### Halloween

 Halloween has been one of our favorites. I recall the
year—the kids were probably seven and nine—we put
on a Halloween party. The highlight was to be a Spook
House in our basement, and I went to great lengths to
plan and direct how it was all supposed to work. (Peeled grapes for
the squooshy eyeballs and all.) But it flopped completely. Nobody
took my "spooks" seriously. Then, as the party wore on, the kids
themselves divided up boys versus girls and invented their own
Spook House, each group trying to outdo the other. I remember
that they even invented a complicated rope pulley that brought a
sheet ghost swooshing toward your face. Things got pretty out of
control—my control, that is—but I learned that some things just
can't be planned!

### Make Up Your Own Holiday

 Some families have even come up with their
own holidays. Suzanne Copeland's crew de-
cided that this year it was time to celebrate
Smokey the Bear's birthday—his fortieth,
apparently.

Says Suzanne,

> On the agenda, a cake shaped like Smokey, tree
> planting, a barbecue with information on fire
> safety and everyone helping put out the fire
> carefully.
> Alex (three and a half) says that the first thing
> we need to do is "go out and *find* Smokey."

## New Twists on Christmas

 As her children grew older and Christmas became less
exciting, Claire Wickens "copied an old trick used at English birthday parties":

> Do you know what the English call "crackers"?
> They're tubular-shaped party favors with a string
> attached. When you pull the string, the
> cardboard cracks and out pop the favors.
> Well, I've never been able to reproduce the
> "crack," but I did manage to stuff toiler paper
> rolls for each of us with a variety of activities we
> acted out together. A funny hat is a necessity; a
> simple newspaper hat with a balloon attached (to
> be blown up upon use) one year, a stocking hat
> another. Then some riddles—one per person for
> the others to guess. Also, each person has to
> perform a stunt. Unlimited possibilities here:
> balancing books on the head, walking with a
> peanut on a knife or an orange between the
> legs.
> This takes some preparation (start saving
> toilet paper rolls months in advance), but far
> less time than Christmas shopping, and it's often
> more appreciated.

A Christmas tradition in the Shannon-Thornberry family serves a practical end. Milo explains:

> Early in December, the children begin asking, "When are we going to make paper?" The project consumes a whole evening and results in every chair in the house being draped with drying "tie-dyed" tissue paper. The corners of tightly folded tissue paper are dipped into bowls of food coloring (colored ink can be used, but be sure it's washable!). The excess is blotted between several thicknesses of newspaper, then the tissue paper is carefully unfolded. Perfectionists (as I was when we started this twelve years ago!) can iron the folds out of the paper.
>
> The resulting creations can be used not only for gift wrapping but can also be taped on windows to make "stained glass" for Christmas.

Almost all of the ideas in this chapter can be enjoyed at any age, or with any mix of ages. But perhaps the most fun for you will be not any one of these suggestions, but a game that you yourselves invent or derive from one of ours. Don't be dismayed by ideas that flop—my Spook House fiasco was just one of many such ideas that sounded great to me . . . but didn't make it. The "misses" are part of the discovery process, too.

## Sources of Fun Games for the Whole Family

Gallagher, Nora. *Parlor Games: Fifty Nifty Diversions—From "20 Questions" to "Get the Guest."* Reading, Mass.: Addison-Wesley, 1979. Recommended by Betty Henry; it's entertaining just to read. (Since it's written for adults—with some sexual allusions—you might want to preview it before buying it for the family.) Lots of clever ideas.

*Animal Town Games.* P.O. Box 2002, Santa Barbara, Calif. 93120. Their innovative family board games encourage cooperation and teach you about the world, too.

*Family Pastimes.* RR 4, Perth, Ontario, Canada R7H366. According to Tom Zink, "Twenty-five cents gets you a catalogue of more than fifty games, puzzles and books. We like to play their Harvest Time board game, in which two to four players try to harvest all their crops before winter comes. Players cooperate to help each other."

# 3

# Everyday Things Families Do

**A**lthough we put our "games chapter" first, we don't want you to think that ours is a game house in which we rush from activity to activity. That's not it. Without the TV dominating our lives, an entirely different pattern emerges. What we do is ordinary, unplanned and unique to us, just as in every family. In this chapter, we try to capture some of this "ordinariness."

According to one language specialist, Americans under thirty have spent on average twenty minutes a day talking with other people since they were two years old—compared with their six hours a day watching television. So perhaps the most dramatic difference that occurs without TV is that people simply *talk* more! Sometimes these conversations are just the daily exchanges that let us know what our loved ones are thinking. Sometimes they are more memorable. Seven-year-old Craig White shares an example from his life: "Every time my grandpa comes over, all my family crams into the living room and it is like "talk hour" at the Whites. My gramps and my father would get into funny arguments about everything in the world. I would learn more in one night with my gramps than I've learned in seven years."

## MEALTIME

Mealtime with young children can sometimes be an ordeal. Janaki Costello's family has developed a simple ritual to bring everyone together in a review of the day:

## The Best and the Worst

 "During dinner, we have The Best and the Worst," says Janaki Costello. "Each family member has a chance to say the best and the worst thing that happened to him/her that day. Examples: Adam, 'My worst was helping Dad pick up branches in the yard. My best was drawing a picture with Mom.' Josh, 'My worst was definitely feeling sick during the baseball tryouts. My best was winning two prizes at the Blue and Gold Dinner.' Jamie (age two and a half), 'My best is sledding.' Heine (Dad), 'My worst was having to make Josh help me in the yard. My best was finally getting the trees pruned.' Janaki, 'My worst was being worried about Adam's cough. My best was going to the Cub Scout Sunday at the community church with Josh.'

"Sometimes we learn revealing things about our children's feelings—what's bothering them or making them feel good or about activities or school events we might not know about otherwise. Kids, likewise, get comfortable with our ups and downs and our willingness to share our feelings and concerns."

Of course, just about any of the word games could be played during a meal. You might try Add-On Stories (chapter two), and Do You Remember? (end of this chapter). And what about taking the time to share dreams around the breakfast table?

## FAMILY WORK AS FUN

### Figuring Finances

 We know that most of the adults reading our book wouldn't consider financial record keeping a way to *enjoy* leisure. Maybe that's because for those of us over twenty it's old hat, or maybe it's because we have a lot of anxiety wrapped up in those numbers and decimal points. But for children, family finances have none of these associations. For them, the world of finances and record keeping is the world of adults—important and challenging.

Let me give you a couple of examples.

*Checks*

In her own games, as you'll read below, Anna has always loved incorporating my old blank checks (unusable ones from accounts I have closed) into her games.

But sometimes I let her do real check writing. I give her the stack of bills and my checkbook. She fills out everything but the signature. All I have to do is look over them and sign. It's great.

When she started doing this, I flashed back to my first checkbook. I must have been a teenager. I recalled writing checks those first few times and being terrified I would put something in the wrong space or otherwise reveal that I was not an old hand in this grown-up world. Just think, I told myself, Anna will never have such silly fears. (Then it occurred to me that by the time she has her own account, everything will be electronic anyway!)

Kathy and Gene Severens have asked, "Why not make it *real?*" Their two children, ages ten and twelve, have jobs—from stuffing envelopes at their parents' office to scraping the bricks in their converted country-schoolhouse home—for which they get paid. Says Kathy,

> They both now have their own savings and checking accounts on which they make deposits and write checks, which they think is an absolute thrill. They each get a bank statement each month, which they check over and file.

*Tax Records*

I always end up at the end of the tax year with piles of receipts I need to organize and record as business expenses. Anna, at ten, took on the job of organizing, recording and calculating my receipts. All I had to do was to give her the categories—travel, office supplies, books/subscriptions and so forth. If she couldn't easily determine where a receipt should go, she simply put it aside for me to deal with later.

It worked. I got her started several weeks before tax day so that she didn't have to rush. She could work on it only until it got boring and then come back to it when it looked challenging again.

Now my dad has convinced me that I must stop just collecting receipts and really get organized with an up-to-date ledger. I think Anna could handle this, too. Maybe I'll pay her for the service, since she needs more spending money now.

### Weighing, Playing

Other parents have made similar discoveries about what looks like just dreary "business" to us adults. Fred Mindlin, who lives with his four-year-old daughter, told me this story:

> The night before last, Lupin and I came home late in the evening, and she began complaining that there was no one to play with. I sat down at my desk to look at the mail—she sat on the desk. I told her I'd love to play with her.
>
> She started fiddling with the letter scale, asking how much different things weigh. We got into trying to put together a combination of things that would weigh exactly a pound, the limit of the scale. We had to do a lot of balancing and arranging of the pile and trading things to get the right combination. But we got the feeling of how heavy a pound is.

Fred's story made me want to go out and get a letter scale. It would offer lots of possibilities.

## CLEANING UP AS A FAMILY AFFAIR

Like household finances, cleaning isn't exactly what one would expect to find in a book about *leisure time*. True, cleaning is not technically leisure, but it can be enjoyable—or at least the aftermath can be.

Since I've never been terribly organized about how the kids share in upkeep, I turned to friends for help. Joan and Alan Gussow came up with a great scheme. Their two boys are now grown, but Alan recalls their cleaning-the-house routine with evident pleasure:

> One time when Joan was away on a lecture trip, I [Alan] realized that it was *our* house, and that *all* of us (kids included) had the responsibility to get it clean. Our house is a three-story Victorian with fourteen rooms, and it was clearly impossible for Joan to clean it all and have it all clean at one time.
>
> So we evolved a plan of action that lasted for many years. On Sunday morning, starting at seven or eight, we would meet in the kitchen and divide up the chores, the rooms, the carrying out of things to be thrown away. We tried to vary the jobs. (This is when the boys learned to clean bathrooms.) Vacuums would go flying, dust brushes, the works. Joan preferred quiet. The rest of us would turn on the radios for music, and the house really jumped. Given the four of us working very hard, it would often take until eleven o'clock in the morning before we were done.
>
> Then, our reward. We would go out to the local diner for a huge breakfast—we could all order exactly what we wanted and as large a breakfast as we wished (and some of those breakfasts were very big, I will say!). And we would come home to a really clean house.

Kathy and Gene Severens and their two children have a similar Saturday morning routine. "Checking off each chore as it's done makes it more like a game." But along with the list of chores, we also make a list of things we'd like to do that day, either alone or with the family. They act as rewards for our work done.

We've noticed that there are chores that young children especially like to do—those producing immediate, visible results. At various ages, Anna has enjoyed taking the squirt-on cleaner and doing a bang-up job on woodwork or making the stove or refrigerator shine.

### Cleanie Meanies

 Linda Young and her kids (ages seven, five and one and one half) have another way of making cleaning into something special and fun:

We do something called Cleanie Meanies, which we copied from a TV ad. We dress up, the kids and I, in bandanas and aprons and run through the house singing funny songs like "Whistle While You Work."

Sometimes we would make up names for the rooms. My room became the King and Queen's chamber. The hallway became the tunnel, full of dangerous alligators. The kids' room was the jungle. We'd put the names on slips of paper and draw to see who got to clean which room. When we got tired of these names, we'd make up others.

And we made up names for ourselves on slips of paper—the Wizard of Oz, Tinkerbell, the Wicked Witch or Cinderella. We'd draw to see who got to be which role. Of course, we could always change, if we didn't like what we got.

It takes an awful lot of energy to clean house that way, so we only do it when I'm feeling energetic. It started when the kids asked why we didn't have a housecleaner like some other families they know. I told them it was because we wouldn't get to do this together. But, I

realized that I don't like cleaning, either. So, we
made it fun.

## Laundry Time Together

 Toddlers and very young children can get a big kick out
of the laundry routine. I remember Anthony loving to
empty the dryer of all the warm, sweet-smelling clothes.
Little kids can also help sort the clothes. The delightful
book *Growing Up Equal* (by Jeanne Kohl Jenkins and Pam Mac-
donald and published by Prentice-Hall, 1979) suggests you slip a
sock on your preschooler's hand while he or she helps fold. The
pretend puppet becomes the folder.

## Dividing Up the Chores

 We all mind housework less if we feel the chores are fairly
divided. Instead of having parents assign chores, Pat
Henry suggests that everyone gets to choose the chores
they prefer; whatever is left over is rotated.

Seven years ago Claire Wickens's three children divided the household jobs up on three cards. Each week the cards were rotated.
They're all in high school and college now, but the system still works
whenever they're home.

## FAMILY COUNCILS

 The idea of regular family meetings sounds good. I wish
I could go back and make that a tradition in our family.
(I think it's too late.) But the Gussows actually did it.
Here's how Alan recalls their family "councils":

> Once a week for many years, we would meet in
> the kitchen. We had a suggestion box, and
> anyone in the family could put in what they
> wanted to talk about at our meeting. It was like

a family town meeting, and everyone was
treated equally (not like Orwell's *Animal Farm*,
where everyone was equal but some people—
animals—were more equal than others). All
kinds of grievances came out, fines were levied,
allowances were discussed, minutes were taken.

These were Alan's memories. Joan added her own note: "As for the
family council—fortunately we did have two adults and two children,
so they could never completely outvote us!"

Andrea Persky has three children. The oldest is six. The Perskys
tried family meetings, too. "Lately, I've let them slide," says Andrea,

and now the kids are asking, "When are we
going to have our family meeting?" In our
meetings we talk about who is doing what in the
coming week. I remind them of their chores.
We review how things are going. If I point out
something bad—like how their bedmaking is
getting sloppy—I also make a point of noting
something good.

We also use the meetings to plan one family
outing each week. We take a vote on what we
want to do.

We also talk about the rules. One of our
rules, for example, is that everyone has to be
dressed and the beds made *before* breakfast. One
of the kids suggested that we change the rule so
that beds can be made after breakfast. We
talked about it. I tried hard to be positive.
Okay, I said, let's try it. So far it's working out
all right. Since one of the children suggested the
change, I think they're all more intent on
making it work.

Linda Young and her husband, Jim, were annoyed by their kids constantly leaving the bathroom a mess after their baths. When they put
the problem on the Family Council agenda, the children helped solve
the problem:

We thought the kids were just being thoughtless. But we discovered that they *didn't know how.* They were overwhelmed by the job. To them hanging up a towel was a big deal, and we'd never shown them how. So we simply put up a little picture chart so that they could see step-by-step what had to be done: (1) towels on rack, (2) water wiped off floor, (3) bath toys put away and (4) clothes in hamper.

That was a year ago, and there's been no problem since. Often what we think are problems turn out to be just a lack of knowledge.

## CREATING IN THE KITCHEN

### On Their Own in the Kitchen?

 The main problem with kids in the kitchen is not with the kids but the parents. It's hard to let go of our turf. What if they break something! Or make an intolerable mess.

Well, the first fear we can conquer with plastic mixing bowls. As far as the mess goes—yes, it's true. But, fortunately, kids can also clean up their messes as part of the privilege of using the grown-ups' place.

Last year Anthony and a friend set out to make a nutritious snack to take to school for a little party culminating the end of a unit on nutrition. They chose the Peanut Butter Log from *Diet for a Small Planet.* I'll include it here because it is the kind of recipe that even much younger children could make with little supervision.

### Peanut Butter Log (one 10-inch log)

*½ cup peanut butter*
*2 tbsp honey*
*3–4 tbsp instant nonfat*
*dry milk (more as*
*needed)*

*½ cup raisins*
*shredded coconut (optional)*

Blend the peanut butter and honey together. Then work in as much dry milk as you need to make the mixture easy to handle and fairly stiff. Knead in the raisins, distributing them evenly. Roll out into a 1-by-10-inch log. Roll the log in shredded coconut. Chill, slice or pull apart. As a variation, just roll the mixture into bite-sized balls.

For a get-together of the contributors to this book, Anna shaped the peanut butter mixture into miniature TVs, using toothpicks for antennae and chocolate chips for dials!

## Basics for Invention

 Kids love to cook because of the fun of mixing and tasting. They get frustrated by the restrictions of recipes. As seven-year-old Benji Rudiak-Gould puts it, "My little brother, Nathaniel, makes his own recipes by adding ingredients 'until there's enough' and cooking it 'when it looks good.' Now, that's the way *I* like to cook. I hate to follow recipes, even my own! So I've tried to teach some of the basic ingredients and their proportions—of, say, cookies—to my kids. With this little bit of knowledge they can add their favorite ingredients or use what's on hand and always come up with something that is at least edible.

### Cookie Basics

Here are the cookie basics that kids can learn by heart: Preheat the oven to 350°F. In two bowls, mix wet and dry ingredients separately:

| Dry: | Wet: |
|---|---|
| 2 cups whole wheat flour | ½ cup oil or margarine |
| 1 tsp baking soda | 1 egg |
| ½–¾ cup brown sugar | ½ cup milk |

Pour the mixed wet ingredients into the dry and mix, using a wooden spoon to blend thoroughly.

Now the fun begins. Kids can add their own favorites:

a teaspoon of ground cinnamon
3 or 4 handfuls of the following: nuts, sunflower seeds, raisins, shredded coconut or chopped fruit (about any dried fruit is good, or fresh, chopped apple), in just about any combination

The more adventurous can substitute ½ cup oatmeal or other flour for the same amount of wheat flour.

Once kids get a feel for how stiff the batter should be, they can add more liquid as necessary to balance the added ingredients.

Bake at 350°F for about 15 minutes, or until the cookies turn golden brown.

### Pancakes and Waffles Basics

Like cookies, pancakes and waffles also lend themselves to the fun of invention. Again, it's a matter of having the basics in mind. Then kids can vary the ingredients and come up with new favorites. In *Diet for a Small Planet* I include a "quick mix" recipe that you can make in large quantities and use for everything from muffins to coffee cake to waffles. If you have this on hand, kids can start with it and just add the liquid plus any extras.

If not, encourage them to learn the basics so that they can start from scratch. This year Anna made waffles for everyone for our family's Easter Sunday brunch. Here's the basic recipe she used, plus some ideas for variations. "Sometimes when I'm cooking," Anna says, "I pretend I'm a chef on television explaining everything I'm doing to my audience."

In two bowls, mix the wet and dry ingredients separately:

| Dry: | Wet: |
|---|---|
| *1 cup whole wheat flour* | *2 eggs* |
| *2 tsp baking powder* | *1½ cups milk* |
| | *3 tbsp oil* |
| | *2 tbsp honey* |

Pour the wet ingredients into the dry and mix. (Little lumps are okay.) Pour about ⅓ cup of the batter at a time onto a hot waffle iron. On ours, the waffle cooks in 5 to 7 minutes.

Substitute ½ cup or so of the following for ½ cup flour:

wheat germ
wheat bran
oatmeal
cornmeal

Note to parents: Using the wheat bran and germ, you can give your children a brief nutrition lesson, explaining that the bran and germ are what are taken out of the wheat to make white flour. But, since the wheat germ contains many vitamins and minerals and some protein, the nutrition of the white flour suffers when it is removed. The bran fiber also aids digestion.

Although it might appear that bran would add to the "heaviness" of baked goods, it actually makes them much lighter.

Returning to the frivolous, Betty Henry invites us to consider a:

## Pancake Zoo

In her household, pancakes have character.

If you fry pancakes in two stages, you can make animal shapes with darker eyes and other features. First position the eyes, mouth, and so on correctly in the pan. Leave them for a few minutes to brown before pouring the rest of the animal over these beginnings.

Letter pancakes can also be made this way. Pour out the letter and after it browns, pour a round pancake around it. Make sure it's made backward so that it's correct when flipped.

In Claire Wickens's family, animal shapes are also a favorite. "But since many don't come out looking as they were intended, a new game arises to imagine what the pancake *does* resemble. But think fast; the pancakes get eaten very quickly!"

## Smoothies

Kids also love to use the blender to whip up new specialties. After-school snacks of their own creation can also be extremely nutritious. The possibilities are endless. When the kids were little, we often had smoothies as bedtime snacks.

Here are just a few of the possibilities:

milk, buttermilk or yogurt (My kids preferred the sweet-sour effect
    you can get using buttermilk or yogurt.)
ice
banana
strawberries
melon
orange juice concentrate (just a little)
egg

For more complicated dishes, where recipes are required, you don't
really need "kids' cookbooks," Molly Sullivan points out. "You can
write your own recipes big and clear for kids, or copy from your
own cookbooks. My daughter, Gabrielle, has her own card file of
recipes written out in a way she can read easily."

As I have talked with other parents, I have learned that some have
successfully gone much further than I in encouraging their children
to be confident in the kitchen. Says Debbie Devney, "My six-year-
old can roast a chicken. Both my kids love to knead bread. (You get
the finest, lightest-textured bread from an angry child.)"

## READING TOGETHER

Among my favorite memories of my children's younger years are
reading together before bed. In chapter four, we focus on reading
activities with toddlers. Here we want to remind ourselves that reading out loud is not just what you do with little kids.

### And Reading Aloud

 Several people have given me this good idea. From Julie
Summers:

We read aloud to one another when one of us is
doing a task that doesn't take a lot of

> concentration, such as food preparation or
> cleaning up. That way chore time is made highly
> enjoyable, as together we climb in the
> Himalayas, explore the Arctic, visit people of
> the South Seas, have a raccoon for a pet and do
> countless other things. Because the medium is
> the printed word, the show can always start
> whenever we want it to.

And Rhea Irvine told us how delighted she was last summer when one of the adults in her household pulled up an easy chair in the middle of the afternoon and started reading aloud one of Grimm's fairy tales:

> His chair was perched at the door to the
> bathroom in which a friend and I were just
> preparing to regrout the tile. Over the days we
> were on the job, we moved to science fiction
> and then to an improvised guitar
> accompaniment. The songs fit the story line . . .
> playfulness *is* contagious.

### Poetry's Pleasures

 Recently my mother gave Anna a book that she hoped would "take"—*101 Famous Poems* (Contemporary Books, 1958). It brought back memories for me that had been all but lost—how I used to beg my mom to read and reread "The Highwayman": "The road was a ribbon of moonlight over the purple moor,/And the highwayman came riding — Riding — riding —" It terrified me . . . but I *loved* it.

And the book did "take" with Anna. For several days, she and I took turns reading our favorites out loud to each other. She particularly liked Wordsworth's "Daffodils." Another of her favorites was Ella Wheeler Wilcox's "Solitude." Now, you may think you've never heard of it. But don't these opening stanzas ring familiar? "Laugh, and the world laughs with you;/Weep, and you weep alone"?

My mom added these reflections on the joys of reading poetry aloud:

When I ran into *101 Famous Poems*, it made me wish that I could go back a few years with my grandchildren, when there were still the precious bedtime reading hours.

When I was growing up, we loved to hear Mama read "The Charge of the Light Brigade" and "The Highwayman" for their drama. When all the day's work was done, we—seven of us—had an hour together around the flickering coal oil lamp. Mama had a very good reading voice—and even as babies and toddlers we responded to the sounds of "The Bells" by Edgar Allan Poe, with its "tintinnabulation that so musically wells/ From the bells, bells, bells . . . /From the jingling and the tinkling of the bells."

This may sound awfully old-fashioned, but why not experiment with reading some of the classics to your children—especially the poems from which lines and phrases have become part of our societal vocabulary? You may be giving your children a treasure. For instance, there are many books on "death and dying"; the subject is popular on the TV talk show circuit. Yet, a poem I learned over sixty years ago speaks all there is for the heart to learn about death:

> *So live that when thy summons comes . . .*
> *Thou go not, like the quarry-slave at night*
> *Scourged to his dungeon, but, sustained and soothed*
> *By an unaltering trust, approach thy grave*
> *Like one who wraps the drapery of his couch*
> *About him, and lies down to pleasant dreams.*

Surely at six years old I did not know the meanings of all the words and images; yet in this poem I learned truths before I was old enough to argue with them. Their solace has carried me through years of losing loved ones to death, of horrible wars and of the danger of wars more horrible.

And then there is simply learning the love of words. Just try for yourself "Hiawatha's Childhood" by Longfellow: "By the shores of Gitche Gumee,/By the shining Big-Sea-Water,/Stood the Wigwam of Nokomis,/Daughter of the Moon, Nokomis . . ."

## WORKING WITH WOOD

  One of the decorations on our back porch is a little flower box that Anna made when she was nine. We set her up with some scraps of wood, nails and a hammer in the backyard, and with a little bit of coaching she turned out a box. Of course, we then had to figure out what to *do* with it. We nailed it to the porch railing and—voilà, a flower box!

## LEARNING FROM NEIGHBORS

Some neighbors of mine have come up with an ingenious way to share time, skills and support. Miriam Hutchins tells this story:

My friend Peggy is an American married to a Guatemalan. She has two children—four and two years old. They all speak Spanish. My daughter Amanda is taking Spanish in an after-school program, but I didn't feel it was a living language for her.

So, because I also wanted to learn Spanish, we started an exchange. One night a week we make dinner and Peggy and her children come over. (Peggy's husband works at night.) Peggy gives an hour lesson to Amanda and her friend Emily. Sometimes the younger ones take part, too. They sing songs, play Bingo and Lotto. If the kids are playing dressup when Peggy comes

over, she'll translate their play into Spanish. And
we try to speak Spanish at the dinner table.
Peggy's kids get to practice their Spanish and
feel good about using their Spanish around their
friends. We all benefit.

## OUTDOOR ACTION
### Walks and Picnics

 For five years, the kids and I lived in San Fran-
cisco at the foot of what is called Bernal Hill.
From the top of the hill, the panorama is mag-
nificent—the San Francisco skyline, the ships
at the docks—and, of course, we always could pick out our tiny house
below.

From time to time, after school, we would put sandwiches in a
bag, drive up near the top and then hike to the very top, a grassy
mound with big rocks jutting out. The fun was finding our favorite
rock, which offered a little protection from the wind. The kids would

*Picnics on Bernal Hill*

scramble over the rocks while I sat and enjoyed the view. Sometimes we pretended we were great explorers.

In *Diet for a Small Planet* (the 10th anniversary edition), I tell about another favorite walk up a hill the three of us made. But we were in Antigua, Guatemala, not San Francisco. I had taken the kids with me for a month of language study. Behind the home where we lived with a Guatemalan family rose a beautiful peak. From the top we could look down on the entire valley. On our first hike up the hill, for the first time, my children saw that just two families owned huge estates (coffee fincas), covering a large portion of the valley. My five-year-old son was shocked: "But, Mommy, that isn't fair! Those people have so much. The people we saw this morning on the way to school were just living alongside the road. They have no houses at all."

Sometimes changing perspective—quite literally—can open us to new insights.

My friend, nutritionist Joan Gussow, tells a story reminiscent of my own experience:

> When Alan was at work and I was going mad talking just to two children too young to have anything much to say, I would just pack up whatever we were going to have for lunch and we would walk down the hill behind the house—just junk woods, cutover stuff, and we would have our lunch among the weeds. Perhaps it's left over from my California childhood, this necessity to get outside as much as possible, especially to eat outside.
>
> We would hunt wild things to eat, wild strawberries, raspberries—even *one* was a great find. We discovered the only morel I ever found on that ratty slope—also ground-cherries and a quince. We also hunted cocoons, though we had little success. I had a passion for moths and butterflies left over from *Girl of the Limberlost* and desperately hunted for all stages.

*Morning Walks*

A number of the contributors stressed the pleasures of enjoying the outdoors during the "off hours"—off to most of the world, that is. Or, so says Debbie Devney,

> Instead of watching Saturday or Sunday morning TV, we sometimes go for walks in the park or on the beach. At nine o'clock in the morning, you can still have the park or beach to yourselves. What a way to wake up! The animals come out to visit. We've met deer, birds, lizards, snakes, crabs, sand dollars, starfish and turtles.
>
> If you're into it, the better part of the picnic breakfast can be packed the night before. We've had the biggest fun, and taken the best "Grandma pictures" on these morning adventures.

*Walks After Dark*

The other end of the day can offer possibilities for walks, too. Most of us don't consider nighttime walks with kids. But park ranger Tim Gordon loves his evening adventures with his toddler daughter, Megan:

> In the evening when I get home from work, we often go to Megan's favorite playground and "spook around in the dark." We watch the night coming down, the stars coming out and the moon coming up. Or often we just watch the afterglow in the foggy sky.
>
> We make up stories in the dark, run and yell as loud as we can. Sometimes we take a flashlight and look for things on the sidewalk.
>
> We've been doing this since Megan was a very little girl. It's made the night a special time for us and the dark a friendly place.

And then there are the "off seasons"—snowy winter when most of us couldn't imagine a picnic. Not so the Gussows. We have just quoted Joan; Alan remembers the wintertime:

> We used to take lots of picnics, particularly in
> the winter, clearing snow off picnic tables in a
> nearby state park. We would laugh and tremble
> when the swans arrogantly demanded to be fed.
> Most people think of picnics in summer
> weather. For us, the best picnics were in winter,
> in snow, on bright blue sunny days.

## In the Garden

 According to a Gallup Poll, 38 million American families garden. So many people associate me with food that I'm embarrassed to admit this—but we're not one of the 38 million. (I fear I travel too much to keep it well tended.) But many of my friends have discovered gardening to be an activity to which even a two-year-old can contribute.

Forest Kan lives in the country, but his advice could apply to city dwellers with yards just as well:

> Every weekend, one day is gardening day for all
> four of us. I've been a collector of tools from
> garage sales. When I realized there are kid-sized
> tools, I started picking them up, so the kids now
> have their own shovels, rakes, picks. We
> delineate jobs they can help with. Even the dog
> is allowed in the garden that day, because it's a
> family affair. The kids mulch and put straw on
> the paths. They rake the mulch off the beds.
> Jomra can dig holes for potatoes and Komishe
> can put the potatoes in. They love playing with
> water, so I have quite a few hoses with
> attachments.

Lindsay and Tom Mugglestone have discovered that even their one-year-old, Abby, can take part in gardening. According to Lindsay,

> Abby will last as long as two hours in the yard if she's had a nap and lunch, and as long as I'm around and available to her. She loves picking up little round things. Right now her thrill is green persimmons that have fallen.
>
> She's also fascinated by the hose, even if it's not on—how it moves. She loves the faucet it's attached to. She'll turn it on and off while I'm watering. She sits and just sprays all around when she's got the hose on. She's not interested in "real toys" when she's outside.
>
> She likes to stack the littlest terra-cotta flowerpots and saucers. She makes collections.
>
> There's one thing about being outdoors—it's always changing. You never get bored.

*Growing Up Green*, by Alice Skelsey and Gloria Huckaby (New York: Workman, 1973), invites you to discover gardening with your children. You'll be introduced to possibilities ranging from a five-foot "farm" to an indoor cactus collection.

## Bird Watching

 Bird watching takes patience and concentration, not the qualities that kids are usually noted for. But Joshua Banner told me about his father's unique approach:

> Our father used to feed birds at the feeder. He set up a system of small rewards to induce us children to watch the birds, too. When we were very little, he would give a piece of candy to whichever child saw a kind of bird for the first time in that feeding season (winter). When we

got bigger, he would give a nickel to the first
one to report a kind of bird new for the season,
and a dime to whoever saw a bird that had
never been seen at the feeder before.

Each of us spent at least a couple hours a
week watching. We got the idea of keeping
records from year to year, and I at least have
become and remain a birdwatcher even though
there is no longer any money in it!

### Cheaper than a Health Spa

 I am a bit of a fitness nut, I'll admit. I'm always trying to
figure out a way to get exercise that doesn't take time
away from other things I want to do. (I am regularly
teased for doing knee bends as I talk on the telephone!)
When the kids were younger, I searched for ways I could get the
exercise I so desperately wanted and be with them at the same time.

After I had finished working, during the longer days of the year,
Anna would get on her bike and I would put on my running shoes.
I would jog just ahead of her. Because we lived on a curving street
then, part of my job was to call out each time I saw a car coming.
Anna then rode onto the sidewalk.

Skates were part of my answer, too. On the wide sidewalks and a
big (sloping) parking lot down the street, we devised any number
of skating games. Sometimes we used a jump rope with which I could
pull Anna along—all the better for my workout. Sometimes we imagined that we were airplanes or trains. From our imaginary cockpits
we would talk to each other through our pretend radios. And, of
course, we played tag on our skates, too.

When I was pooped out, sometimes I would just sit on the stoop
and count so that Anna could race against herself. I'd say, "Bet you
can't make it to that blue car and back before I count to ten." I would
count and she would skate as fast as she possibly could. Then I would
up the challenge. "Bet you can't do it in eight!"

To my great surprise, I also learned to play catch with Anthony.

My painful memories of junior high school when I was graded on pitching and throwing skills—and I couldn't even hit the target, much less get a high score within the target—made me doubt that I could really use a glove and catch a baseball. But I did pretty well. Last year I even learned to throw some pretty mean grounders to help Anthony train for third base. Even Anthony will admit it—sometimes.

Other parents have made similar discoveries—that they can enjoy getting outside and doing things so often reserved just for children. From the kid's perspective, Gabriel Wachob agrees. He and his dad developed a routine of going out bike riding together each weekend: "I love racing with my dad and riding with the other friends that sometimes come with us. I like it because it gives me a sense of total power. I can do it almost anytime I feel like it."

## PETS—NOVEL AND NOT

 Caring for and enjoying pets fill many happy hours for adults and kids. But many people who don't have yards or big homes wonder how to fit a pet into their lives. Our friend Peter Barnes and his sister, Valerie, came up with a perfect answer to this constraint—a box turtle named Spotty that was part of the family for more than ten years. Peter told us,

> We found Spotty on a road in Pennsylvania and wondered whether he would adapt to New York City apartment life, but he did. He was the perfect pet. He didn't make any noise. He didn't bite and was always pretty friendly. He would eat out of our hands and let us play with him. Unfortunately, he loved high-quality meat—veal and very lean hamburger. Fortunately, he didn't eat much! But what Spotty loved the most was being in the warm, steamy bathroom when someone was taking a bath. In the warmth, he'd really start to boogie.

Even when Valerie left for college, our parents
would take Spotty to visit.

Sara Stein's *Great Pets* (New York: Workman, 1976) is a good in-
vitation to novel pets (as well as ordinary ones). Why not a sala-
mander? A mouse or a snake? Stein not only introduces you to the
care of all these pets but explains how to build homes for them, too.

## KEEPING FAMILY HISTORY

### More than a Photo Album

 We all love looking through picture albums—so why not
expand them to include other special reminders of moments we never want to forget? For most of us, the problem is just getting ourselves to sit down to do it. Kathy
Severens has a suggestion:

When the kids were born, I began a tradition of
making a family photo-scrap book every year
after Christmas. The children love these books.
Often Anna [the same age as our Anna] would
rather sit with me and go through a couple of
photo books before bedtime than read a book.
Now the kids have started making their own.

### Do You Remember?

 Just reminiscing about shared experiences is
one of the great rewards of lifetime relation-
ships. I often try to re-create in my mind exactly what the kids were like when we lived
in New York and some precise scenes from trips we've made together. It's fun to ask them how much they remember. I was amazed
recently that Anna at ten could vaguely outline the floor plan of the
house we lived in in Guatemala when she was only three.

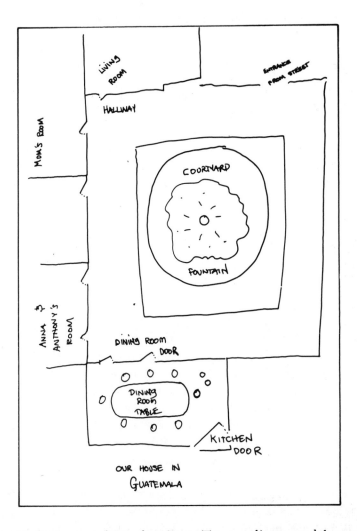

LIVING ROOM

ENTRANCE FROM STREET

HALLWAY

MOM'S ROOM

COURTYARD

FOUNTAIN

ANNA & ANTHONY'S ROOM

DINING ROOM DOOR

DINING ROOM TABLE

KITCHEN DOOR

OUR HOUSE IN GUATEMALA

Eugene Nelson and his daughter, Tamar, discovered how much fun it is to remember, too: "Sometimes, while driving or at home or on hikes, we'll relive exciting trips we've taken. We discuss certain parts of the trips. Sometimes we make a game of trying to remember as many details as we can—which cafés we stopped at, what we ate, what paintings we saw in museums and so on."

## VISITING PARENTS AT WORK

 I remember so vividly going to the airport to visit my dad's workplace as a child. He was a meteorologist for thirty years with the U.S. Weather Bureau. I loved the sound of the teletypes whirring. I loved the big maps and the instruments the weather forecasters use to collect rain samples. But most of all I loved just *being* in the grown-up world of my dad.

Even if you think your place of work is nothing much to see—no teletypes or rain gauges—it will probably hold equal wonder in the eyes of your kids. Because I work now with a not-for-profit educational institution—the Institute for Food and Development Policy—it's been easier for me than for some parents to acquaint my kids with the world I work in. In Anna's words,

> This summer I am doing volunteer work there, three days a week. I can stuff envelopes, sort zip codes, distribute the mail and do lots of other jobs. And they let me type order codes into the computer. It gives me a feeling for how life is for people going to work everyday. Even though I don't get paid, I enjoy doing it because I know I'm helping out my mom and the people she works with. Maybe there's a volunteer organization in your neighborhood where your child might ask about doing similar jobs? It beats sitting home all summer!

Some parents, even those in terribly demanding jobs, manage to include their kids sometimes. Meadow Goddard, age fourteen:

> The way I spend time with my mom is go to her work when she's working a double shift at Children's Hospital. I go on rounds with her. Sometimes I help wheel the IV's into the rooms, and I get to talk with the patients. I really like that.

Writing this chapter was perhaps the most challenging because it is the "everyday" things that we—like so many people—take for granted, often don't value very highly and then forget. So some of the best ideas in this chapter required real effort on our part to remember. And many came from people who, when asked what their families do when the TV is off, said, "Nothing. Nothing interesting." But when we probed, we discovered that what they might take for granted is delightful and original to others.

While it's easier to remember and to tell about the special games and other occasions, this chapter's theme is truly the heart of our book—for it's the "everyday things" that develop a new richness and diversity in the many hours we discover once the TV is off.

## Resources for Enjoying "Everyday" Time

Haessly, Jacqueline. *Peacemaking: Family Activities for Justice and Peace.* New York: Paulist Press, 1980.

McGinnis, Kathleen and James. *Parenting for Peace and Justice.* Maryknoll, N.Y.: Orbis Press, 1983.

*The Mother Earth News Almanac of Family Play, Pastimes and Pursuits.* Mother's Bookshelf, 105 Stoney Mountain Road, Hendersonville, N.C. 28791.

Sisson, Edith A. *Nature with Children of All Ages.* Englewood, N.J.: Prentice-Hall, 1982.

# 4

# Enjoying Time with Toddlers and Young Children

Until Anthony was four years old, and Anna one and a half, I stayed home with them. Several days a week, I took them to a baby-sitter down the street so that I could study and write, but I was mainly an "at home" mom. I relish my memories of those years, considering myself very lucky to have been able to savor that ever-so-fleeting time. Yet I remember, too, the emotional challenge of spending so much time in constant demand and without adult stimulation.

I started working full-time in 1975. I then began to appreciate the other kinds of challenges—of juggling one's energy and attention between children you love and work you love.

I hope this chapter will speak to both kinds of challenges.

One general word of advice. Forgive me, please, if this sounds trite. But remember, when living with toddlers and young children that this time will pass before you know it. So don't wish it away! Take advantage of your toddlers. Let them give you an excuse to slow down to their speed and to do silly things you wouldn't other-wise do.

This is our longest chapter, in part because we feel it is our most important one—for it's as toddlers that patterns of TV watching get established. And as parents of toddlers it's awfully tempting to get into the habit of using TV as the regular baby-sitter. We can rationalize by telling ourselves that instructive programming like "Sesame Street" is good for our kids. But early childhood educators are increasingly dubious—even the best TV programs distract toddlers from the primary way they develop, which is by touching, feeling, moving, manipulating and interacting.

We don't want to make you feel guilty for an occasional use of the electronic baby-sitter (although, as we've said, many parents have found removing it altogether to be the easiest approach). Rather we hope our experience and that of others in this chapter will demonstrate that it *is* possible not only to keep one's sanity but actually to enjoy our little kids more without TV's domination.

(Just a reminder: In every chapter—especially chapter two—there are ideas for toddlers and young children. Please don't overlook the possibilities there, too.)

## SURVIVING "THE PITS"

 I called it the late-afternoon and early-evening "pits." The kids are fussy. Energy and patience are low. Dinner has to be made. The house needs picking up.

For parents who work full-time, it's even harder. You're exhausted. You haven't seen the kids all day. You want to focus on them, make dinner and recover from work all at the same time.

So naturally the TV offers the answer! Just turn it on and kids are out of your hair. You can relax or cook in peace.

Are there other ways to survive "the pits"?

For at-home parents, part of the answer is to anticipate it and to short-circuit the syndrome. Knowing that my lowest energy time is always late afternoon, I tried to plan my days with the kids so that I could get an energy pickup then.

### Walks of Discovery

 We often took late-afternoon walks. When Anthony was about six months to a year and a half, I used to carry him in a simple sling carrier that put him on my hip and distributed his weight to my shoulders. This way he was in front so that I could talk with him. I much preferred this to either stroller or backpack. As we walked, I could point things out to him. (I also loved early-morning walks when the air was fresh and the town still sleeping.)

Lindsay Mugglestone's dog, she says, gives her just the impetus she needs to get out of the house for walks with her two-year-old.

> Sometimes we just walk from our front door.
> But other times we drive to a different
> neighborhood—one we've never been in before,
> just to see new things. As we walk, we always
> talk about what we're seeing. Sometimes we
> look for matching colors or textures: "I see a
> blue house—and here is a blue flower. There is
> a shiny car and here is a shiny light. There is a
> prickly vine. What else might be prickly?"

### Dinnertime Downs?

 Well, dinner *does* have to get made. But how can we enjoy cooking with toddlers underfoot? One is to include your toddlers in your kitchen activities. Suzanne Williams adds this idea:

> Why not let your child read to you while you fix
> dinner or clean up the kitchen? Katie loves to
> entertain me. It's good practice for her and no
> trouble for me.

A large plastic container of assorted uncooked beans and various small plastic measuring spoons keeps Betty Henry's toddler occupied while she's cooking:

> Beginning at about eighteen months, Mara has
> spent happy hours sifting the beans through her
> fingers and measuring them carefully into
> different piles and bowls. As she grows older, I

will mix in some uncooked noodles so she can
sort the mixture into piles according to shape,
size and color.

(As Betty points out, it's important for an adult to be around to
make sure the beans don't end up in noses or ears.)

Another approach might be to let your little tots do their own
parallel "cooking." Lisa Van Dusen's mother let her become the
"spoiled leftovers chef":

My mother used to prop me on a stool in front
of the kitchen sink with the huge salad bowl and
as many containers of past-their-prime food as
possible. I'd stir, add water and "cook" up a
storm with food that otherwise would have been
thrown away.

Andrea Persky, mother of three young children, offers another
idea:

I taught the children how to set the table and to
do simple chores in preparing the meal—like
measuring the water. They loved it! And I felt
better because I knew they were doing things
more valuable than sitting in front of the TV.

Suzanne Copeland adds that in occupying little kids before dinner,
the centerpiece can become the focus of their creative attention:

. . . flowers, candles and beyond. (Just let the
kids choose. It will be wonderful.) Making little
bouquets or decorations for each place is fun,
too. You might even want to let them choose
the music!

Faced with the same predicament of trying to cook dinner with a
four-year-old underfoot, Donna Michelson came up with this idea:

> I am going to the library and ask the librarian to
> help me find some good children's stories that
> are particularly dramatic to tell. I want to
> commit four or five to memory. Then, when
> Megan wants to be around me while I cook, I
> can tell her one of the stories. It relaxes us
> both.

Dinnertime Downs can include not just the stress of trying to cook
with hungry toddlers underfoot but dining time, too. Theoretically,
dinnertime should be relaxed—we keep telling ourselves—but too
often it can be just the opposite. With a new baby plus a three-year-
old, Kristine Brown has faced the frustrations of meals with toddlers
and offered this idea:

> We call them our "unfortunately, fortunately"
> stories: "Unfortunately David cried all morning,
> fortunately he took a nap later, unfortunately he
> woke up, fortunately I had a pillow to put on
> my head!"

Kristine's suggestion is reminiscent of the Best and the Worst
dinnertime-discussion gambit in chapter three. (Both break through
that "How was school? Fine" dead end.) Chapter two also includes
a number of simple word and guessing games that could calm everyone down at mealtime. One that Kristine's family thought up: "I'm
thinking of something red and good to eat." Endless possibilities.

## A Special Activity in Reserve

 You're trying to make dinner or pick up the house when
you get home from work. Or you just need a break. But
how to keep the kids occupied so that *you* can get
collected?

If you're lucky enough to have the space, why not keep special
play or craft things in or near the kitchen—*an activity that's reserved*

*as a special treat just for that time you need to concentrate or relax.* Consider the craft counter Kate Olsen tells us about in chapter six.

## Set the Stage

 Kristine Brown, a former teacher and now the mother of two preschoolers, offers this possibility for encouraging your children's independent play. "Setting a stage" becomes a theme for imaginative play:

> One of the most successful "stages" we set was a hospital. In a room, or corner of a room, set out a place to lie down, some sheets, a pillow. And something that can be a stethoscope, bandages and tissues. Add paper and crayons for get-well cards. Perhaps some flowers, books and quiet games.
>
> Kids especially enjoy being the patients and therefore have to rest a lot, but they also enjoy playing different roles: doctor, nurse, visiting friend, parent, pet. It's fun when an adult joins in, especially as the patient—but it's not necessary to the activity.
>
> Other possible stages? Construction site, radio station, TV studio, acting stage, train or bus station, airport, circus, supermarket, school or day care, or the beach.
>
> By adding or changing props, kids stay interested for at least a week.

## BEDTIME WITHOUT TEARS (I mean mine, not theirs!)

 When Anthony and Anna were little, our bedtime routine was one of the most enjoyable parts of my day (usually). I discovered that if I started early enough (so that I still had some energy and didn't feel pushed to get them to sleep for their own sake), the routine relaxed me, too.

Reading was a big part of our ritual. Each night they each picked a book or a chapter for me to read. We alternated who got to go first.

Donna Shultz, with three kids (ages one, five and six) tells of her family's storytime:

> We have a special chair that fits us all
> comfortably, and what generally happens is that
> by the time the last story is read, the first two
> children are asleep in the chair. Regardless, after
> reading time is over, it is bedtime and they go
> with no hassle. They get very upset if we are
> out late and don't get a story. When asked, they
> all prefer storytime to watching television.

While there were always certain books we would read over and over again, Anthony and Anna loved having new books read to them regularly. Suzanne Williams has hit upon a good system for using library books to extend your family's repertoire:

> At the library I let Katie choose the books she
> wants. (And I mark the due date on my calendar
> as soon as I get home.) We have a special box
> for Katie's library books right in the corner of
> the dining room. It's covered in bright green
> Contact paper and labeled Library with blue
> tape. It holds over a dozen children's books.

### Storytelling

  A break in one's routine can sometimes teach. Remember our trip to Guatemala? With few external resources available to us, I discovered some internal ones. We had no TV, no radio the kids could understand—and we had very few books in English. So, if we were to continue our bedtime ritual, the stories had to come from me. What? I'm not a storyteller—all my books are nonfiction! Just the thought intimidated me. But I began to wonder what it would be like to try to make up a story on the spot right out of my head.

So I began. I was astonished. I would just start with a character and a vague idea of the situation, and things would start to happen. A plot, of sorts, would start to emerge. I would have been too self-conscious if any other adult had been listening, but the kids really liked my stories. And I felt so proud of myself.

So we recommend that you close the door—that way you won't have to wonder whether you sound foolish to any other adult—and just let your imagination go with your kids.

I remember asking a good friend, Bill Ayres, what he enjoys doing with his toddler daughter. The first thing that came to his mind was the ongoing banter they have about a chipmunk character he made up more than a year ago. The imaginary chipmunk immediately became a real friend to his daughter; together they come up with all sorts of adventures.

So, try it! (And remember, storytelling is not just for the benefit of little kids. See chapter five.)

### Let the Kids Tell It

Children can tell stories, too. Leila Graves, age eleven, says that sometimes, "my mom tells a story, and then I tell one like it. Then we talk about how my story was similar or different."

Joe Devney adds, "Bedtime is my special time with the kids. But they all take turns reading—even the five-year-old. He tells the story from the pictures."

### Lie-Down Time

I honestly don't remember how it began, but from the time that Anthony and Anna moved from cribs to their own beds, we developed what we called Lie-Down Time. Lie-Down Time is that ten minutes or so at the very end of my children's day when I would lie down beside each of them in

turn (alternating each night who got me first). During these ten minutes each child had my absolute, undivided attention. I never planned
ahead what would happen. Sometimes we would just lie there in the
dark and talk quietly about events of the day. But over the years we
discovered some favorite Lie-Down-Time activities:

*The Mystery Back Writer*

 It started when Anthony and Anna were just learning the
alphabet. With one finger I would "write" a letter of the
alphabet on their backs for them to guess. Then, as they
got older, I wrote simple words, one letter at a time. They
would guess each letter as I wrote it and then have to put the letters
together to make a word. In our most advanced stages, we moved
to whole sentences, which they would have to put together, letter
by letter.

*Draw My Face*

 My grandmother lived with us when I was very small. I
used to go into her room and beg her to "draw" me. While
my eyes were closed, my grandmother would take the
eraser end of a pencil and lightly outline all my features—
with brushstrokes for the eyebrows and hair lines. It tickled a little
bit, I remember, but it relaxed me completely—and knowing my
face was the total focus of my grandmother's attention made me feel
very special.

With my own kids at Lie-Down Time, I would often just use my
finger as my imaginary pen. I would ask Anthony or Anna what they
wanted to be—a clown, a princess, a butterfly or an elf. Then, with
their eyes closed and bodies relaxed, I would draw the lines on their
faces to make them into their fantasies.

*Dead-Drop Game*

 This idea may sound too simple to be fun, but Anna loved
it. It's a challenge, and perfect for bedtime because its
whole point is relaxation. Moreover, it helps a child to
become aware of body tension, consciously noting the
difference between relaxation and muscle contraction.

I would lift Anna's arm above her body and ask her just to let it go completely limp so that I was holding its total weight. When it felt relaxed, I would let go so that her arm fell to her chest. It was easy for both of us to tell whether it really fell with all its weight or whether she was holding on to it. We kept repeating the game until she really let it drop with all its weight. Part of the fun was never knowing where her arm was going to land, once she really gave it over to gravity. Sometimes she liked to be the one to hold my arm up. We were both amazed at how heavy it was when it was truly relaxed.

*Tepee Sleep*

  The Copelands occasionally turn bedtime into a real adventure:

We threw together a tepee out of some bamboo (which we are fortunate to have growing in our backyard) and four old sheets. This gets set up on the backyard lawn, and we sleep in it overnight. Sometimes we read Indian stories by flashlight before nodding off.

## "LET'S GET PHYSICAL!"

  The greatest discovery I made (for my own benefit) as a parent was that my kids could teach me how to have fun. I'll confess—I've always been a rather serious soul. The worry line on my forehead dates back to kindergarten. But our kids can allow us to let go of our inhibitions . . . if we can muster the nerve to put aside our "this is how it should be's" or "will I lose my 'grown-up' image?" reservations. If we parents maintain our distance for fear of losing our authority, we can miss so many opportunities to truly *enjoy* our kids. I am certain that we can enjoy doing silly things together without losing their respect. And in the plain fun we can share, lifetime bonds form.

When the kids were about four and seven, we tried yoga postures before bedtime. (There are now several paperback introductory yoga books especially for kids.) I can't say we were ever very meditative. It was more of a contest to see how many of the postures we could do. But it was fun away.

## Desperation Dance

 Anthony was sometimes a fussy baby. This was especially true during what I called "the pits." It seemed as if almost every day about five o'clock in the afternoon he'd start to cry. I became desperate, until I discovered that there was one cure—dancing.

I would move the couch out of our way and roll back the rug and put on a good rock 'n' roll or pop record. With Anthony on my hip, away we would go. Somehow I particularly remember bouncing around the living room to Paul Simon's "Mother and Child Reunion."

As is true of many of the ideas in this section, I got some good exercise as a bonus. And Anthony did stop crying!

## The Galumph Dance

Tom Zink and his son, Jesse, often play music on the radio or cassette player in the mornings while they do other things.

Sitting in his high chair for a midmorning snack, Jesse hears the music from the other room and taps his hand on the arm of the chair.
Sometimes I scoop him up in my arms and we dance around the living room, doing pirouettes, slides and "galumphs" on the hardwood floor. A "galumph" is a single gallop step taken by a bigger person holding a smaller person in his/ her arms. The *galumph* is the punctuating sound at the end of the step as the carrier and the carry-ee bounce down together with a *Ga-a-a-a-aLUMPH!*

His thirty pounds quickly get heavy, so our *pas de deux* are brief but exhilarating.

## The Flying Lappés

As the kids got a little older, our favorite evening activity was often creating our own acrobatic tricks on the living-room floor. All you need is a soft carpet or big foam pads. Here are some of our inventions:

*Leaning Tower of Pisa*

With me flat on my back, Anthony or Anna would perch with his or her bottom on the soles of my feet extended up in the air. The "leaning" part was the fun. I would move my legs slightly forward and backward or sideways, making it a little scary for the rider. The "leaning tower" was defi-nitely a good one for strengthening my legs. (You see my selfish interest in all this.)

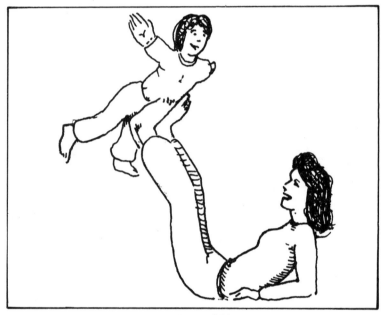

*Leaning Tower of Pisa*

### Merry-Go-Round

 In Merry-Go-Round we were in the same positions as in Leaning Tower of Pisa except that after *they were up on my feet*, I would move my feet and legs around in an up-and-down circle mimicking a merry-go-round (whereas in the earlier version my legs moved slightly sideways or back and forth).

### Cannonball

 You need a little more room for this one! Again, I would lie on my back, but with my legs curled in close to my chest. Anthony or Anna would lean over me with their pelvic bones against the soles of my feet. I held their hands. I then rocked back and forth—1–2–3! On the count of 3, my legs would uncoil. I would let go of their hands and they would fly up into the air like a cannonball. They landed (usually) on their feet. The higher in the air, the more fun!

(No one ever got hurt—the kids really only went a few feet in the air, but it was a real thrill nonetheless.)

### Bucking Bronco

The name says it all. I was the bronco, an angry one at that. With the appropriate snorting and huffing and puffing, my job was to dislodge a squealing rider from my back.

Kevin Cadogan said that he and his dad played what they called Rodeo from the time he was five until he was eight. They took the game a step further than we did. "I would hang on as long as I could," he said, "and we would time how long I stayed on."

### Pyramid

Our show-stopping act was Pyramid. Sometimes it would take us a long time, but Anna actually learned to balance up there on top, and I am sure my back and shoulders became much stronger as a result of this one. Anthony and Tim's drawing shows you our proud feat.

## LETTING GO—CRAZY FUN

Recall that I suggested we let our toddlers and young children give us permission (as they say here in California) to be silly. Our "acrobatic" tricks represent something of that process for me. I must have looked pretty silly stretched out on the floor, or snorting like a bronco. Here we'll share some other families' fun in just being silly.

*Human Pyramid*

## Hop on Pop

From Janaki Costello:

The three kids try to get Dad's head to touch the ground so they can win. Dad must get all three of their heads down at one time. The kids usually win.

## Fun Fights

Alan Gussow, whose sons are now grown, remembers their favorite Fun Fights:

Getting down on my knees, bending over,
making myself into an inverted u shape, the
boys would crawl through me, as though I were
a bridge. The bridge got smaller and smaller
each time they went through, and finally one
would be "caught." Then the other would jump
on me to free his brother. It was fun to squeeze,
nudge and touch.

Roughhousing had special meaning also in Molly Sullivan's family:

Wrestling has always been a favorite activity in
the family. But it acquired real importance when
Frank joined our family. Having a stepfather
was a huge change for everyone. Gabrielle was
nine and Isaac was eleven. Frank found that
through friendly, exuberant wrestling, bonds
could be formed. Some of their happiest times
during those first years were wrestling. I think it
was because you show who you really are—how
sensitive, caring and strong.

### Snooglehoogle

Elaine Magree and Toby, four years old:

Toby says, "Snooglehoogle." I pretend I don't
hear him. Then he says it again and I turn into
an outrageous character and chase him through
the house. I cackle, shriek, tickle and threaten
to eat him. He tries to get away. He says,
"Vaminos," to stop anytime he wants.
   Toby has a sign on his door that says,
"Snooglehoogle," which an adult friend he was

staying with made for him. That shows how much he likes this game.

## Collapse

Tom Zink's family has no TV and is thinking of starting a "support network" for other families raising kids without it. He says that we like "to just forget the clock for a few minutes and relax, playing a game like Collapse":

Collapse is an after-supper game. Mom and Dad "collapse" on the floor; it's been a hard day at work, and supper's been a real "scream." So we lie down, prop our feet up on the counter or the refrigerator door and wait for our two-year-old son, Jesse, to fetch a couple of pillows from the living room. We slide the pillows under our heads, and the game begins.

Jesse plays, and we are the props. He climbs over us, bounces up and down on our after-supper tummies and props puzzles up on our legs to piece back together. He has a great time. We get to relax and have nothing to do but pay attention to him.

Sometimes after supper, Mom or Dad collapses on the living-room couch—alone. The game of Collapse cannot be played alone, so Jesse and the uncollapsed parent sneak into the living room to pounce on the unsuspecting loner. Jesse often starts giggling too soon, but that's the fun of sneaking in and starting the living-room-couch version of Collapse.

In this version, Mom and Dad lie on the couch with their feet next to each other's head and Jesse climbs over us, between us, from one end of the couch to the other. The by-product is a gaggle of giggles.

## Pickle Family Circus (the name of a San Francisco Bay Area circus)

 When my kids were little, jumping on the beds (and from bed to bed!) was one of the all-time favorites. The Galarza family adds its version:

> The oldest boys—ages seven, five and three—like to play Pickle Family Circus, especially after taking a bath. I am the announcer while they, taking turns, do acrobatic tricks on our king-sized bed. Whoever is not having a turn is the audience, and we cheer and applaud after each show. This is especially fun at Halloween time, when we have makeup in the house and they become clowns.

## Dirty Laundry

 Sally and Gordon Lake's four-year-olds love it:

> One child volunteers to lie on the floor completely covered by a blanket. One of us or our other child says, "Oh, look at this. This must be a pile of dirty laundry." We slowly start to feel the pile and say, "Hmm. This feels pretty hard. This is funny laundry." We stretch out the comments and the touching and the tickling as long as the kids are having fun.

If another book might help you come up with more such fun ideas, try Betty May's *Tickle Snug Kiss Hug: Exercises and Tricks for Parent-Child Fun* (New York: Paulist Press, 1975).

## QUIET GAMES

### Draw Me a . . .

 Larry Jordan's kids, Amy and David, have a favorite game. They give Larry drawing instructions: "Draw me a pencil." Or, "Draw a sad baby." And Larry obliges. The kids love to see the pictures. We've included some of Larry's artwork to inspire you!

*Draw Me a . . .*

## Blindfolded Drawing

Anna, Anthony and I have had fun seeing what we come up with if we close our eyes and draw. Isa Cohen offers her version:

About two times a week my mom and I draw. Our favorite way is when one of us shuts our eyes and draws. After about thirty seconds, the other person takes the paper and tries to find a picture. One day we were in the kitchen at about the time of sunset. I had closed my eyes and doodled, and my mom had found a bunny. I could tell my mom was having fun by the sparkle in her eyes.

## GAMES OF FANTASY

### And What Will You Have for Dessert?

When Anna was five to about seven years old, one of our favorite after-dinner activities was playing "restaurant." She was the waitress and cook. I was the patron. She would draw up elaborate menus with astronomical prices.

I would walk in and seat myself at a "table." I would have different personalities—sometimes an elegant lady and sometimes a very gruff and demanding one. I would order from the menu and always have some comment about the quality of the cooking. She would write out my check and sometimes use the toy cash register to ring up the bill.

Part of the fun was naming the restaurant. It almost always had a different silly name.

### Now You Can Rinse . . .

The Lakes' twin four-year-olds prefer to play "dentist." "It's best to do this in the kitchen or bathroom, because water may spill," they warn:

For supplies, you'll need a chair, table, cup with water, bowl for spitting, paper napkin to cover the patient's shirt and a flashlight. The child, or patient, sits in the chair. The "dentist" tucks the napkin into the patient's collar, looks into her mouth with the flashlight and then says, "Take a little water and rinse your mouth out. Spit into the bowl."

The dentist can pretend to fill a tooth or clean the teeth. We keep this up until somebody wants to change places. You can expand this game with a pretend waiting room and the dentist calling patients in.

## INDOOR ACTION GAMES

### Pillow Throw

Anthony, Anna and I invented this game on one long evening when we were alone together in our home in Hastings-on-Hudson, New York. Anna was not yet three, and Anthony was five. I sat in the middle of my bed with a bunch of throw pillows. One at a time, each of them would dart across the room from one doorway into the bathroom. I would try to hit the moving targets with my pillows. It wasn't easy.

In another version, Anna and Anthony would take turns jumping from my dresser onto the bed. Sitting on the floor or in a chair nearby, I would try to hit them with the pillow while they were still in the air. If I hit them, I got a point (or something—it was pretty loose, score-wise), and if they caught the pillow, they got the point.

## Wet Rag

 A game of nerves! We took turns standing in front of a wall or closed door. One of us would throw a damp washcloth at the "target." The object was to get as close to the target as possible without hitting the person. The challenge for the target was not

*A game of nerves!*

to flinch. If you flinch, you lose. (By the way, the cloth was never wet enough to spatter so it didn't mess up the wall.)

### Train for a Rainy Day

 Claire Wickens, mother of three now-grown children, recalls their favorite rainy-day activity. "We called it simply Train," she recalls:

All the children brought into the family room every conceivable chair or stool or ottoman or box that could support their bodies yet safely be climbed over. A delicate antique or flimsy stool was omitted from the project. Now came the imagination and cooperation in lining up these obstacles in train-line fashion.

For an engine or caboose, we chose something quite different, something to crawl *under*—often a large upside-down box with cutout doors, or a rug humped up to make a tunnel, or large pillows or chaise-lounge pads supported in some fashion to give something to crawl under or through.

Now the train was ready for testing. Each child must climb from one object to the next all the way down the line. Common sense would clue a parent into carefully observing to make sure that that old high chair third down the line is not going to tip over when the toddler blunders over it. This aspect of danger (in the children's minds) provided a special sense of challenge and adventure.

The object, of course, is to go from one end of the train to the other. Going both directions provides variety. So does changing the order of the kids, as the youngest always wants to be first

at some point and the others (opportunity for
patience and consideration here) must follow.

By the time the train is rearranged several
times, put into an S shape or even circular (for
smaller rooms especially), you've passed away an
entire rainy morning providing both fun and a
great deal of physical exercise for the brood.
While the children put away all the chairs
(understood from the beginning), there's time to
fix lunch for the now-hungry ones.

## Anytime Egg Hunt

The Henry family doesn't restrict the fun of egg hunts
to Eastertime. Why not substitute any little, favorite
objects?

We frequently hide little Fisher-Price people all
over the house. This is a great activity when
neighborhood children are visiting. They love to
take turns doing the hiding.

## Treasure Hunts for Little Kids

Sally Lake describes how she organizes treasure hunts for
her four-year-old twins:

I put something in a paper bag—anything from
a new book to a funny picture—and hide it. I
then make up clues, usually four, that require *no*
reading. The clues are either crude drawings
(I'm no artist) with an X marking the hiding spot
or a picture cut from a magazine with an X
drawn in at the appropriate spot. The clue

usually shows the sofa, the big chair in the living room, the bathtub, kitchen table, the refrigerator or a child's bed.

I have the children go into a room and shut the door while I hide all but the first clue. (Each clue is folded a number of times because they *love* unfolding it!)

With great enthusiasm and animation on my part, I ask the children to come out of their room and I hand them the first clue. I stand by offering encouragement in case they can't figure it out. They *race* from clue to clue until they find the brown-bag treasure at the end of the hunt.

I use almost anything for the treasure, including new socks. Last week one of the children made four clues and organized a treasure hunt with no help from me.

Betty Henry's family has its own version of Treasure Hunt. The Henrys use pictures, too, drawn on 6-by-8-inch paper, as the clues. "We have built up a collection of pictures so that our average Treasure Hunt now has up to thirty hiding places," says Betty.

## BATHTIME FUN

Bathtimes are among my happiest memories of Anna and Anthony's early years.

### Soapsuds Sculpture

Once the kids' heads were sudsed up with shampoo, the fun began. I would mold the foamy white in all sorts of becoming styles. Devils' horns were a favorite, but we had other elegant "dos." We kept a mirror hanging on the wall by the tub so that Anthony or Anna could see how hilarious they looked.

*Soapsuds Sculpture*

## Bubble-Up

 Betty Henry's two-year-old, Mara, loves this one:

Just take the washcloth and lay it on the water.
Reach your hand under it to lift the center,
forming an air pocket. Then grab all the edges
together under the water. Babies and little
children love to squeeze the cloth and watch the
bubbles.

## Back Design

 Here's another soapy game. I would soap Anna's back
into a rich lather, which I would then smooth over the
whole back. With my fingertips, I would draw pictures
in the smooth lather. Sometimes I wrote letters and words
for her to guess.

### Snow Melt and Other Thrills

 When Anna got a little older, we had fun experimenting with different water temperatures. The game was to see how cold she could stand the water poured over her head. (This was *her* idea!) We had names for different temperatures, and I would mix hot and cold until I got just the right concoction. We had "snow melt" and "spring rain," I remember. She would squeal with delight.

### Just Enjoying the Water

 The kids also just enjoyed having soothing warm water poured over them, using a big plastic container we kept handy. Or sometimes I took our long sponge, soaked it in the water and then put in on their shoulders, letting water stream down their backs.

Some of our best talks were during these long baths.

### Out-of-the-Bath Antics

 From Betty Henry's experience:

Once out of the tub, our children loved—say, between the ages of two and six—being wrapped in a large towel and rested over the parent's lap. We'd pretend to play complex concertos, singing as we'd play.

## FANTASY FUN

In chapter five, we highlight the delights of imaginative play—kids alone and kids with adults. Here we want to include Elaine Magree's experience with her four-year-old. With very young children, fantasy play can be a special way of communicating needs.

### Fred the Cat, Where Have You Been?

 With just a little encouragement, most kids love to become fanciful creatures. Elaine tells about Toby's delight in pretending:

Toby has multiple personalities: Mr. Puppy Pie, Fred the Cat, the Baby, Toby's Dirty Brother. He comes into the room and acts like one of these. And I respond accordingly.

"Meow, meow."

"Oh, it's Fred the Cat. Where have you been?"

"New York."

"My, you've made a long trip!"

Then sometimes Toby is transformed into a different creature.

"Whoof, whoof."

"Oh, Mr. Puppy Pie. I'm so surprised. Fred the Cat was here just a second ago."

And on and on. But sometimes I use the playacting to encourage Toby to ask for what he needs. When he starts whining or asking me to do things that I know he can do for himself, I'll say, "Oh, the Baby's here. How are you, Baby?" I don't say this as a put-down. I say it as if it were great to see the baby again. This allows him to just cuddle up and be nonverbal. Sometimes this is exactly what he needs. He's a kid who often acts a lot older than he is, and sometimes he needs to act younger, too.

## BEACHES AND BABIES

 When Anthony was a toddler and Anna was a baby, we spent several weeks during the summer at Cape Cod. Anthony's thrill was to stand with a parent at the water's edge. We would wait for a big wave to come and then grab him up just as it was about to hit. He loved the excitement of the cold, foamy sea splashing over us.

But what to do with Anna? If we put her down in the sand directly, she started eating it and got sand in her eyes and diapers and became pretty uncomfortable. So we turned our little backyard plastic wading pool into a beach playpen. We carried it down to the beach, inflated it and put her in it with all her toys. She could watch the goings-on and had a great time.

Another innovation from that summer was Anna's sleeping arrangement. Instead of lugging a crib all the way to Cape Cod, we took a hammock. We strung the little hammock over our bed, and whenever Anna woke up, we just gave her a little shove and the hammock rocked her back to sleep.

## NO-PLANNING EXCURSIONS

 Remember that outings that seem the most mundane and ordinary to an adult can thrill a child. Sometimes on weeknights, after a long day at their offices, Sally and Gordon Lake go on an evening outing with their preschoolers.

Here is a list of some of their short excursions:

Riding a couple of stops on the local train and back
Watching planes at the commuter airport near their house
Going to the bowling alley and watching the bowlers
Going to the elementary school and looking in the windows and playing in the playground

## "KILLING TIME" WITH KIDS

 I *hate* the expression "killing time." Every moment should be precious—no?? But I use it purposely here. For there *are* those hours we'd like to kill—waiting, for example, at the doctor's office, the airport, the bus station, or the government office. These can be torturous times with impatient, squirming youngsters. (Most of us find it hard enough to wait, even when we're alone.)

But, I learned, if I could stop focusing on how annoyed I felt about waiting and start focusing on the opportunity to be with my kids (in a situation where I couldn't be pulled away to dirty dishes or the telephone), then good things began to happen.

Sometimes we'd play the simple "naming opposites" kinds of games mentioned in chapter two. Larry Jordan, whose drawings for his kids we included in this book, says that the Draw Me a . . . game (page 90) can be a good one for interacting with his toddlers at a restaurant when it seems like the food will never come.

### How Observant Are You?

 One day waiting at the doctor's office in San Francisco, Anna and I came up with a great waiting game. One of us closed our eyes (and promised not to peek). The other then began making up questions like:

"What color are the walls?"
"What animals are painted on the wall in front of us?"
"What color is the floor?"
"What color dress does the lady sitting directly in front of us have on?"

I found it interesting to learn how oblivious I can be of my surroundings! Anna often did better than I. In any case, this game could go on for some time—the more crowded the office, the more possibilities for "observation" questions.

### I See!

 Claire Wickens's family made up another good waiting game. It could work in similar situations— such as "waiting in the car for

Daddy to come out of the stores," says Claire:

> Each person takes a turn. From where he is
> sitting in the car, he spots something identifiable
> and says, "I see a cat sleeping in the window,"
> or whatever. Then everyone tries to find it.
> When everyone has located it, it's the next
> person's turn.
>     Sounds too simple? Well, it worked many a
> time for my family and also made us more
> observant.

## The Andersons Enjoying Each Other

 How hard it can be to escape the pervasive cultural message that being with our kids is a drag. That's why I so
loved Mary Anderson's story. "It will illustrate the value
of our TV-less life," Mary says.

> Last weekend I flew to Portland on business and
> took Michael (age six) and Rebecca (age
> eighteen months) with me to visit my ninety-
> five-year-old grandmother. My conference was
> over at four, and the plane left at 8:30. The
> airport was fifteen minutes away.
>     The baby-sitter expressed condolences for my
> upcoming airport "ordeal." It was no ordeal—it
> was delightful! Michael, Becca and I watched
> planes land for an hour, trying to be the first to
> spot an incoming plane and to guess which
> runway it was heading for.
>     Michael insisted on carrying all the hand
> luggage (traveling light made this possible).
> Becca then decided *she* would carry *her* luggage
> (a huge basket of diapers).
>     Dinner stretched out for a pleasant hour.
> Michael and Becca then romped and

roughhoused for an hour. Very pleasant,
enjoyable, entertaining!

And yet, at some point, I looked around and
was surprised to see so many people bored and
restless waiting for their planes with pained,
glazed expressions!!

Our life is simple, filled with work and
responsibilities and yet rich, rewarding and
entertaining—and the entertainment is
spontaneous and effortless. Why should we have
someone else do our laughing and loving for us?

It's important to remember that the parents of the toddlers in this
chapter are no different from you. We *all* have those days when just
surviving the next hour with our kids feels like a major accomplish-
ment! (And is.)

## Additional Ideas for Life with Babies and Young Children

Hagstrom, Julie, and Joan Morrill. *Games Babies Play and More Games Babies
Play*. New York: Pocket Books, 1981. Lindsay Mugglestone has also found
this book helpful.

Munger, Evelyn Moats and Susan Jane Bowdon. *Childplay: Activities for
Your Child's First Three Years*. New York: E. P. Dutton, 1984. Lindsay has
enjoyed this book with her daughter Abby, the tiny gardener you met in
this chapter.

Sullivan, Molly. *Feeling Strong, Feeling Free: Movement Exploration for Young
Children*. National Association for the Education of Young Children, 1834
Connecticut Avenue, N.W., Washington, D.C., 1982. Molly has contrib-
uted several ideas to our book, including the story about playful wrestling.
Her book is intended for teachers, but parents can find many good ideas
here.

# 5

# Especially for Kids: Imagine Yourself an Actress ... Dancer ... Radio Announcer ...

*I'm alone, and the TV is off. There's a thing my mom calls creative thinking. It sounds pretty weird, but my mom's a therapist. Well, anyway, creative thinking is just when a kid sits and stares off into space and thinks. And for some reason you don't get bored.*

JULIAN PRINDLE

*To me TV would be a good way to spoil my doing-nothing time. People who don't give it to themselves by design often seem to end up having it forced upon them by accident or illness. In my doing-nothing time, my mind is free to wander as it will.*

JULIE SUMMERS

Growing up on TV, we do have a hard time believing that *doing nothing*, just giving one's imagination free play, could be enjoyable. We see ourselves as the targets, positioned to receive entertainment, not the generators of our own delights. And in the process our imaginations become perhaps the most seriously abused victims of TV.

One symptom of this abuse is a shift that early-childhood educators observe in children's play: TV appears to have taken over our children's imaginations, even when they're away from the set. "The traditional doctor, nurse, police, fire, family role playing has been replaced with TV movie heroes such as Luke Skywalker, Princess Leah, Mr. T, the Dukes, He-Man and so on," reports Harriet Dyer, the director of a nursery school in Farmington, Connecticut. "Imitative play has taken over imaginative play." Imaginative play requires invention—making up characters and thinking up plots. Just mimicking TV super-heroes has little of this dimension. It's loud and aggressive behavior—what Ms. Dyer calls macho play.

So there are no Mr. T's or Luke Skywalkers in this chapter. Here instead are some tantalizing glimpses at just how much fun it can be to use little but . . . imagination.

## KIDS PRETEND

### Yikes, Alligators!

 When Anthony and Anna were little, one of the most fun games of all was pretending that the floor was a sea of horrible monsters. Sometimes alligators. Sometimes snakes. The object was to travel around the room without touching the floor—I mean, falling into the alligator pit. You could build bridges where necessary. And you were allowed to help each other get across the treacherous gaps between table and couch.

### Building Your Own House

  Blankets and boxes. And sometimes card tables. That's all we needed to make indoor houses in which my brother and I could play for hours. With blankets and a chair or two we could add on annexes and little nooks and crannies for favorite dolls and toys.

Anthony and Anna used big cardboard boxes—the kind that appliances come in. We cut out windows and decorated the outside with watercolor.

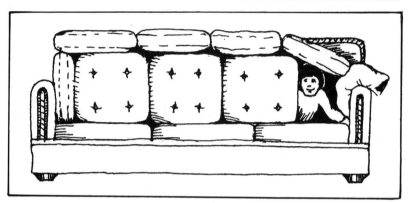

*Couch Fort*

## Dollhouse on a Shelf

 Dollhouses always seemed like such a great idea for fun. As a child I had a rather ordinary metal one. So I wanted Anna to have one that was really special. Two Christmases ago, my friend Peter and I bought a kit and put together the most elegant two-story colonial mansion. We spent many hours assembling and painting. Yes, it is gorgeous and has adorned the dining room for more than two years. But I'll bet Anna has spent a total of one hour playing with it!

So I had to laugh when a child at Berkwood Hedge School in Berkeley came up with this: "One time I just started a dollhouse on an empty shelf." Betty Henry also told us how she and a friend, at fourteen, spent a delightful week's vacation from school converting a four-shelf bookcase into a dollhouse, replete with handmade furniture, rugs and curtains.

## Making Faces

 When Anthony and Anna were about three to six years old, we had lots of fun with making up our faces using colorful (and washable) face paint—the kind that actors and clowns use.

We would go through various "periods"—with hearts (on the cheeks and forehead) or butterflies or clowns. The kids loved making me up the most. (Making adults look silly is definitely a favorite activity of kids.) I can still remember forgetting that I had been made up and then getting the most terrific surprise the next time I looked in the mirror. Or giving someone else a shock when I would answer the door with one of my many faces.

## GET INTO THE ACT

 Anna and her best friend, Justine, introduced us to the fun of playacting. They got inspired one night after we had just seen a local community production of *The Kind Lady*. How important, I then realized, it is to expose our children to live productions of the dramatic arts if we want their imaginations to soar.

I've been impressed that my kids (who aren't known for long attention spans and who loved the glamour of *Star Wars* and so on) have been attentive even through some quite serious plays—*Mother*

*Courage* and *Raisin in the Sun*, for example. The realness of live theater can be just as captivating as the glamour of the special effects of TV and cinema.

In Anna's words:

> First we would simply come up with a story plot
> and then we'd act it out for Mom and Peter,
> improvising as we went along. (Since I'm two
> years younger than Justine, sometimes I'd have
> to whisper to Justine, "What do I say *now*?" But
> that didn't matter.) Of course, simple costumes
> gathered from Mom's closet added to the fun.

In encouraging her kids' dramatics, Suzanne Copeland discovered that just a slight elevation really "goes to their heads":

> Put them a step or two up and the show begins.
> Why not put a piece of plywood over your
> sandbox, or make the porch a stage with the
> audience seated below?

## Setting the Scene

 Having one group make up a difficult, funny, embarrassing—or whatever—situation for the other group (kids or adults) to act out can lead to some hilarious moments.

In this vein, your family might want to get *The Magic If* by Elizabeth Y. Kelly (Baltimore: National Educational Press, 1973). Written for the beginning drama student, it includes lots of takeoff points for dramatic skits. In one, for instance, you must pretend that you are a teacher's helper preparing a Halloween party at school. You've placed plastic skeletons, jack-o'-lanterns and creepy fake bugs about the room. Then a boy comes in with a real spider! And before you have a chance to do anything, he's put it on the teacher's chair and the other kids start coming in. What do you do?

In chapter four, we included other ideas for "setting the scene"—a hospital, for example—for little kids' play.

## Brown Bag Theater

 This is *not* a lunchtime entertainment. It's a fun way to stimulate imaginations. You simply fill paper bags with random props—a playing card, a whistle, a feather duster, a mismatched pair of socks, the sports section of the paper.

Hand the bags to the teams. Or two kids might just collect their own random props, exchange bags and take it from there! The idea is to build a plot around the assorted items.

Rhea Irvine has had fun with the Brown Bag Theater on camping trips, where there are no special props available: "We just used the things you can pick up in the environment—a Band-aid, a pine cone, a wooden spoon, a bandana, a package of tomato soup!"

## Putting on a Show

  Elaine Magree tells of the special version of playacting that her four-year-old son, Toby, and his friends love:

At our house, Putting on a Show means that the kids go into a room and make up a story. From our costume box they grab scarves and whatever else they can find. But then sometimes they don't know what to do with themselves. So, I suggest that they draw pictures of their story— with a beginning, middle and end.

Now the fun begins. I "read" the story, using each set of pictures as my inspiration, while the kids act it out. (One point I impress upon them is that each has her or his own version of the

story. There's no right or wrong way. So they
can't change one another's story.) So sometimes
the story might get acted out three different
ways. Of course, they can't go three sentences
without cracking up.

Another way that Elaine encourages Toby in the art of pretend is
that often when he comes home from school and starts to tell a story
about what happened that day, she'll ask, "Do you want me to act
out the other person in the story?" Toby loves this. "He corrects
me and shows me how to do it right."

No doubt coaching his mom on how to play someone else helps
Toby learn to see his experiences through the eyes of others.

### Make Up Your Own TV Show

Says Tamiko Harris, age thirteen,

My family makes up its own TV shows. During
the week a member of my family—my brother
or sister—will write down some event that
happened at school, or maybe at home. Then
they break it down into roles. When the
weekend comes, everybody in the family has a
line to say. And we make up our own TV shows
this way.

If a fight happens, it helps to act it out, just to
show how foolish we looked. One time my
brother and I had been fighting over my bike. I
hit him and he hit me and we were both crying.
My mom suggested that we act it out. I played
him and he played me and we acted out how it
all happened. We ended up giggling and solved
it.

Simple costumes add to the fun of dramatic skits. Sandra Cohn and

Mark Kannett (with a seven- and a one-year-old) told us how they "keep a costume trunk in the basement filled with odds and ends of false noses and moustaches, men's overcoats, old ties and shoes, capes, Halloween costumes and face makeup. The possibilities for parades, plays and general silliness are endless."

## Go to Court

 Pat Cody tells of a different kind of pretend game that was the favorite in her family:

It began because my late husband's father was a would-be lawyer who couldn't afford law school. His profession as a leaser for the gas company in West Virginia brought him into contact with lawyers and courts. When Grandpa came to visit, we would play "court," and he was always the judge.

We would all choose a part: prosecutor, defense lawyer, plaintiff, defendant, witnesses. We would make up the offenses, usually civil ones like breach of promise, who gets the apples dropping over the fence, landlord-tenant disputes, but sometimes we did criminal cases.

It's a form of theater, of course, with a ready-made structure, and our kids really got into their roles. They also learned something about the adversarial system, common law, debate, public speaking.

## THE MAGIC OF WORDS

### Dramatic Reading

 We had never thought about dramatic reading as a fun possibility until we started working on this book. Then one night, looking through a book of scripts from old radio shows, I ran across the script of Orson Wells's "Invasion from Mars." I started reading it out loud and I couldn't stop! Before I began reading, I had told my family that when it was on the air, many people believed it was real. They laughed at me. But after I had read only a few pages, they began to understand why.

Gene Novak came up with another good idea for a very dramatic reading: *The Tell-Tale Heart* by Edgar Allan Poe. It helps, he suggests, if you cut out beforehand any unnecessary words, such as "he said."

## Storytelling

Storytelling engages the imagination of the teller and listener alike. Whereas TV leaves little to the imagination, storytelling lets the listener supply the visual images.

Today, there's a big boom in the old-style art of storytelling. It's not just for little kids; big kids and adults are enjoying it, too. You can buy records and tapes of people reading stories aloud, as well as of storytellers telling tales from memory. The latter are harder to find, but a good source is the National Storytelling Resource Center, Box 112, Jonesborough, Tenn. 37659. They sell records and tapes through mail order and put on storytelling workshops, festivals and performances all over the country.

To get started, you might want to order Nancy Schimmel's *Just Enough to Make a Story: A Sourcebook for Storytelling* from Sister's Choice Press, 1450 6th Street, Berkeley, Calif. 94710. It is a short course in storytelling and lists lots of good stories to tell and read aloud for all ages. It includes a long list of folktales (with "many active heroines, which are not so easy to find in children's books," says Nancy).

## DANCING JUST FOR FUN

Most of us think we have to go out somewhere to dance. But why not just turn on the rock music and roll back the rug? One of Anna's friends, Sara Schuchert, told us with great delight how her dad seems so "proper" to other people, but when he is at home with her, they do "Daddy and Sara" dances, and he "really acts silly . . . and let's go!"

After going to some Jazzercise-type classes together, Anna, Justine and I also discovered the fun of just putting on a rousing rock 'n' roll record at home and taking turns at leading the others in simple exercises.

Gwen Greene has elaborated on the idea with her children:

> At Christmastime we play a beautiful version of the *Nutcracker Suite* and dance around in lots of space with lacey curtains draped over us. The children and I love it. The lacey curtains just fit the music.

## OR BE WHATEVER YOU WANT TO BE . . .

### Why Not a Radio Announcer?

 One of the most overlooked toys is the tape recorder. As so often happens, we made this discovery out of sheer desperation. Earlier I mentioned I had taken the kids to Guatemala with me for a month in 1977 when they were tiny—just three and five years old. I wanted to study Spanish and thought they might benefit from being in a foreign culture. Basically, the trip turned out great; but I'll never forget the few days they were sick. There we were all day alone together in a bedroom in the home of virtual strangers (we boarded with a Guatemalan family) with nothing to do! So we pulled out the tape recorder I had brought to help me study. We ended up recording our own hysterical version of Snow White and the Seven Dwarfs, complete with sound effects and all.

In more recent years, both Anna and Anthony and their friends have enjoyed pretending to be radio announcers, making up commercials and programs. Anna likes to record herself practicing the piano, too.

### . . . Or a Comedian (on the answering machine)?

 One night well into writing this book the three of us were home together on a Friday night. To my dismay, both Anna and Anthony just moped around. They even used that awful word . . . *bored*. "What are we going to *do*?"

I took a deep breath. Repeating to myself the advice I wrote into the first chapter, I just relaxed.

And what happened? Well, Anna and I ended up going out to browse in a bookstore. I found a cut-rate edition of a book by an author I had been devoted to twenty years ago. Anna didn't find anything. But we had fun looking at the picture calendars and just "hanging out."

When we got back, we found Anthony stretched out on the floor of my study talking into the answering machine. He'd found a pursuit more addictive than the slot machine. The two of them spent the next *three* hours (no exaggeration) trying to get the funniest, cleverest, most outrageous message onto the machine.

For example, one version had both of them talking to each other:

ANTHONY: Hello.

ANNA: Hello.

ANTHONY: I got it.

ANNA: No, I got it.

ANTHONY: Hang up, Anna, I was expecting a call.

ANNA: I was, too. You hang up.

ANTHONY: You never get any calls anyway, so hang up

(*Pause*)

ANTHONY: Hey, wait a minute. It doesn't make any difference anyway. We're not even here! So just leave your message after the beep, and we'll get back to you.

### . . . Or a Clothing Designer?

 I can recall drawing my "dream" clothes when I was about Anna's age, but last year she and her friend Justine went the next step: They designed a whole line of clothing and even came up with their own designer label—Peaches 'n'

After drawing and then coloring several dozen outfits (and pricing them, too!), they put them into a special notebook, almost like an order catalog. A year later, Anna still gets pleasure from looking through the drawings.

## . . . Or a Clerk? Or Budget Manager

 Anna's ongoing game of imagination involves coupons—the kind that come in the shopper newspaper and in all sorts of catalogs we get in the mail. Anna:

I collect coupons. Sometimes it seems like I have thousands! Every once in a while I like to go through them and sort out the ones that have an expiration date. Sometimes I ask my mom to pretend she is making imaginary orders from the booklets of coupons I put together.

I use a real sales pad (with carbon) we got for eighty cents at the stationery store. I love writing all the order numbers and calculating how much it all will cost.

Even younger children enjoy playing with coupons, filling in the blanks with imaginary names and addresses.

Once, on a day off from school when her friends were all tied up and she wasn't sure what to do, Anna pretended that she was twenty years old and getting her own apartment for the first time:

> I used catalogs to buy the things I would need
> to set up housekeeping and to plan a weekly
> budget for food, rent and so on. I asked my
> mom what would be an average income that I
> might be able to earn when I am twenty. I had a
> lot of fun trying to make it come out right.

And I think she learned something of how hard it can be to make ends meet on a limited budget, too.

## . . . Or Zoologist?

  "A great tool/toy is a big magnifying glass," says Julie Summers:

> Older kids/adults will appreciate the greater
> magnification of a hand lens—it's a little harder
> to focus than a magnifying glass. You can get
> them at lapidary stores and college student
> stores. They give a new perspective on most
> anything, but are especially revealing of flower
> parts and insects' features.
>
> There is another world to be discovered by
> filling a widemouth glass gallon jar (free from
> many cafeterias and restaurants) with pond water
> (almost any stagnant puddle will do) and
> observing with a hand lens. The book *Animals
> without Backbones*—a classic found in many
> libraries—will help answer questions about the

little critters. A bit of green water plant and fish food will keep it going.

## . . . Or a Mapmaker and Park Keeper?

 Our friend Lisa Van Dusen grew up at the edge of Detroit near a creek:

What I loved to do most was map the creek. It was my special territory. I named everything— the meadows and special landmarks, like the tree that hangs over the river. I even measured the level of the water to see how it changed throughout the year.

I thought of myself as the official observer— sort of the custodian of the creek. I think I was inspired by *Harriet the Spy*. With my note pad and flashlight and measuring devices, I'd stalk my territory for hours. I loved it.

We should add that today Lisa still loves the outdoors and is an avid gardener and backpacker.

## . . . Or a Doctor's Office Manager?

 This is another one of Anna's inventions she can play for hours. It's actually quite complicated because she has a number of imaginary doctors, patients and rooms:

I thought of this game one day when I was really bored but I felt like typing. So I got out the old portable.

I sat there for a little while and slowly in my

**DR. FRANKLIN**   Children's
                   +        Doctor
                   Adult 's
    Name _____

Medication:

☐ Check-up          110.00 on card 75.00
☐ Pain in head           variable
☐ Pain in leg (s)        variable
☐ Pain in chest          variable
☐ Pain in _____        variable
           other
☐ Measles           50.00 on card 25.00
☐ Chicken Pocks     115.00 on card 85.00
☐ _____ other

Card # _____ Regular Dr. _____

Cash ☐ Credit card ☐ _____ Check ☐
other _____

Dr. Information:
  Blood type:
  Additional Information: _____
  _____

Had for _____ Age _____

Billed to _____ _____
                        customer
TOTAL: [$ |    |  ]      [_____]
                         [_____]

_____
  signiture

head I put together the pieces of how to run a
doctor's office. I got out a pad of paper, pen and
the kitchen timer. I set it as high as it would go.
I used it to tell me when the patients went in
and out.

I pretended the office had five doctors. I
would talk to each patient and get their name
and which doctor was theirs. I found out if
they'd be willing to see a different doctor if
theirs was busy. If a doctor was busy, I'd put a
check by the name. I wrote down the time each
patient went into the office. Each visit was five
minutes. So when five minutes was over, I
crossed out the patient's name.

The fun was keeping track of the whole thing
and knowing what you were doing, especially
when so many people were coming in that I had
to make a waiting list!

Another version of the doctor's office didn't
require a typewriter. I just wrote up a form the
patients had to fill out and then imagined the
different patients coming in.

(Be sure to save your old checks from any account you've closed.
They add a lot of "realness" to games like these.)

## . . . Or Travel or Ticket Agent?

 Anna loves to make up games that she can play either by
herself or with a friend. She especially likes games that
require making charts and keeping records. She has made
up a special box with all her equipment—tape, a stapler,
a ruler and an old hand calculator. In her words,

Whenever I get bored, I come up with ideas
about jobs I could pretend to do as a travel
agent. I get out a globe and a pad of paper. I

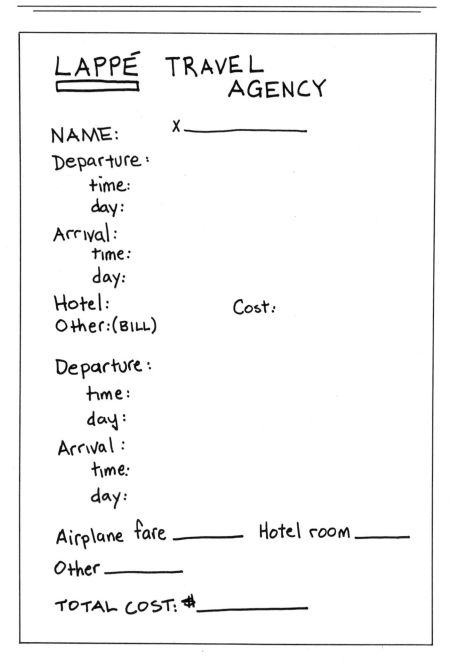

LAPPÉ   TRAVEL
             AGENCY

NAME:        X_____

Departure:
    time:
    day:

Arrival:
    time:
    day:

Hotel:                    Cost:
Other:(BILL)

Departure:
    time:
    day:

Arrival:
    time:
    day:

Airplane fare _____  Hotel room _____

Other _____

TOTAL COST: $_____

NAME:

Flight #:

Cost:          Infant ☐   Adult ☐   Child ☐

Source of pay:          ,(#)

Round trip ☐   One way ☐

Gate ___   Terminal ___   Seat Row ___ ___

X _____   [_____]

    SIGNITURE

LUGGAGE:

Wieght:

Identification #(s):

Item (s):

Food ☐   Breakable Possessions ☐

Paper Documents ☐   Beverages ☐

Flammable Possessions (highly) ☐

Dangerous Possesions ☐   If YES list

    1. _____

    2. _____

    3. _____

Medication ☐   If YES list

    1. _____

    2. _____

    3. _____

> spin the globe and, with my eyes closed, point
> to a place. The first time I ended up somewhere
> in Australia.
> Then I start to fantasize a dream vacation
> week if I had to take it in Australia. I look up
> cities in our atlas to see where the imaginary
> clients could stay and fill in all the information
> on a special form I made and copied.

One way to make the game even more fun and—dare we say—
educational is to get travel brochures from the airlines or a nearby
travel agency for the countries you would especially love to visit.
Older children might even get an outdated master airline schedule
from a travel agent. With it, you can plot out elaborate trips to exotic
places, considering both cost and convenience.

Anna has another related game:

> I pretend I'm the ticket agent at the airport.
> That requires another form, including baggage
> and flight information.

One aspect we particularly like about virtually all the activities in
this chapter is that they can be done entirely by kids, alone or with
friends. Or, they can include adults as either participants or audience.

# 6

# Art in Everyday Life

If you are like me, you're suspicious of books that assume we are all "artistic" underneath our inhibitions. All we need to do is discover our inner talents. But I *know* I'm not artistic. True, in my mid-twenties I went through my watercolor-and-weaving period, but it didn't last long. All I have to show for it are some card-woven belts and two watercolors that made it to my mother's kitchen wall. I can't now believe I even did those.

Nevertheless, I have learned that even those of us who have little artistic talent can help bring art into the everyday lives of our families.

## MAKING ART EASY

The most important thing is making artwork *no big deal*. We can discover ways to integrate artwork into the routine of our lives.

When Anthony and Anna were younger, the house we lived in had no dining room. So the family virtually lived in the kitchen. We would get home from work and school about six o'clock. As I cooked dinner, the kids sat around the kitchen table, sometimes doing homework, but more often drawing. Anthony, especially, could sit for an hour or so totally wrapped up in his pencil drawings. He loved detail. His masterpiece, we all agreed, was a drawing of a Civil War battle in which he had put more than one-hundred precisely drawn figures, each with a uniform of appropriate color.

Anna, on the other hand, was strong on color and form. So having lots of colored pens handy could keep her happy, too.

We kept all our art materials in the pantry off the kitchen. This way the kids could just pull them out themselves as I cooked. Other parents have come up with similar ideas.

## The Crafts Table

  Kate Olsen tells about her daughter's "crafts table" for her three children:

In the breakfast room, adjoining the kitchen, they built a counter along one side, with shelves underneath for all sorts of art materials— crayons, felt pens, scissors, paste, different types of paper, Scotch tape, chalk, stencils plus some other crafts from time to time, such as supplies for sewing, embroidering and so forth.

Sometimes a particular project, such as making valentines, spills over into the dining room, so they keep the dining room table set up for valentines for the weeks before Valentine's Day.

Our daughter says that the crafts table is not just a place for longer projects but becomes a spare-moment activity place, too, where one can put in a few minutes or more while waiting for something else to happen—just as switching on the TV might be for other children.

One big plus is that it is near the kitchen, where our daughter is apt to be working, so that she gets to be in touch with what is going on, for comments, appreciation and so on. We grandparents like the things they send us, made at the table.

But, of course, you don't have to build a special counter like Kate's daughter did; what's important is just creating an atmosphere where kids feel it's okay to have their stuff out and be messy if necessary. Doug and Karen Goodkin, my children's first music and art teachers, respectively, let their "big, funky" coffee table become their four-year-old's art-and-crafts table. "We just turned it over to her," Karen told me. "The main thing is just to keep a space where kids are in control."

### Valerie's Box

 Valerie Jordan, a psychologist and mother of two pre-schoolers, has come up with a simpler version of the crafts-table idea.

Annoyed by the kids' crafts materials scattered about, she came up with the idea of providing a box with a lid for each of them. (Each is about the size of a shoe box.) The reduce-clutter idea turned into something quite special for the children. They keep their tape, scissors, coloring pens and other treasures all in one place— all their own.

### Cut-and-Color Box

 Suzanne Copeland came up with another version—one devoted to all sorts of things with which to build pictures. It should be big enough to hold pieces of cardboard, photos, scraps of any kind, sticky stars, dots and so on.

### Paper-a-Plenty

 Since I'm a writer whose style is to do many, many drafts, we are never short on scratch paper. We keep it in a special pile so that the

kids can grab a piece whenever the spirit moves them. If you don't generate a lot of scratch paper, what about bringing home from the office the copy paper with "goofs" that collect beside every copying machine? This way you don't have to worry about the kids wasting it.

Karen Goodkin also keeps all the bits and pieces of gift wrapping paper for her daughter's artwork. They add color and texture to many projects.

## BUT WHAT CAN I MAKE?

Here are some activities that you may want to try out.

### Simply Sewing

 When Anna was eight or nine, I taught her how to use the sewing machine. The only difficult part, I found, was teaching her to thread the machine. The rest is really a matter of attention.

She didn't feel ready to tackle making clothes, but she had lots of fun making little doll-size pillows out of fabric scraps. She uses cotton balls for stuffing.

She also invented a new art form on the sewing machine. Using many different colors of thread, she sews designs on paper—big spirals, some beautiful borders and some geometric designs.

Debbie Devney, a dressmaker herself, adds this idea:

> I always have an abundance of scraps. The grown-ups cut out squares, and the kids sew them into long or short strips. We've made patchwork quilts, pillows, doll clothes and lots of other things in this way. We sold some of our things at a consignment shop. We even made enough to finance a visit to Grandma in Ohio.

Gene and Kathy Severens, both lawyers, live with their two children—Anna (age ten) and Alexander (age twelve)—in a converted country schoolhouse in Nebraska. Kathy is a skilled weaver and seamstress:

> We bought Anna her own real sewing maching when she was nine—an old, sturdy Singer for $30 that works better than mine. Her machine sits beside mine. Kids want to do what adults do. She sews when I sew. She cuts out a pattern when I do. She sews clothes like I do. I find it easier for me to help her if I'm working right beside her without standing over her head.
>
> We have the same method for weaving. Anna and Alexander have their loom which sits right beside my loom. They learn a great deal from watching and love doing what I'm doing.

## Photo Dolls

 Here's a novel idea that comes from the Henry family—the people who gave us Incongruous Images (page 34).

Have everyone—neighbors and friends, too— put on swimsuits and stand individually with arms and legs apart from their bodies and photograph them. The pictures must be taken in good light with no visible shadows, and bodies should fill as much of the picture as possible. (There's a delay while you get the pictures developed. Polaroids won't work because they can't be cut.)

When your pictures come back, cut out the

people and you have a *real person* paper doll.
Now the fun begins—designing new clothes and
new "images" for them. Just draw and cut out
clothes as you would for any paper doll. We
have outfited our baby (five months old at the
time of her first photo doll—so we had to hold
her standing up) as Little Orphan Annie, Mara,
M.D., Miss America, a spaceperson, a tree, an
opera singer and so forth.

We have a separate box for each person. They
make great birthday presents—just remember to
take the birthday person's picture a few weeks
in advance.

## Newspaper Silhouettes

A giant version of Photo Dolls comes from Sally and
Gordon Lake:

We tape several sheets of newspaper together
and lay them on the kitchen floor. One of the
children lays down on it, and we trace his or her
entire body on the paper (not very neatly!) and
then we cut it out and hang it on the wall.

No doubt kids could have a lot of fun decorating their own sil-
houettes. In *Peacemaking: Family Activities for Justice and Peace* (New
York: Paulist Press, 1980), Jacqueline Kennedy suggests a variation:
To celebrate a birthday, why not tape the birthday person's silhouette
on the wall and then invite family and friends to fill it in, noting the
special qualities they like about him or her? What a special present
to hang up and to enjoy all year.

## Furnish the House

 Debbie Coyle directs a parent-cooperative preschool. She's offered us some of her children's favorites.

Just put a large piece of paper on the floor—a couple of opened-up grocery sacks taped together would do. Mark off rooms in a house, letting the kids decide where the bedrooms, kitchen, bathroom and so on are. Then, with scissors and paste, they can use magazines, old catalogs and furniture sections of old newspapers to furnish the rooms.

Once the "house" is furnished, the kids might incorporate Photo Dolls for even more fun.

## Plasticine Creatures

  Remember, please, that I am not an "artistic" person! So that means that anything "craftsy" I can do I'm sure anyone could. Sculpting is an example. How could *I* make anything out of clay? I thought. But the kids really loosened me up.

I remember one day in particular. Anna was at a friend's house. Anthony and I were home by ourselves without a lot of energy. So we sat down at the kitchen table and pulled out the plasticine (the relatively new kind that comes in really vivid colors) and started making a parade of bizarre animals.

There were lizardlike creatures with red spines, and camellike creatures with blue humps. There were floppy-eared fellows and those with pointed spines like nothing I'd every seen before. Those friendly creatures stayed on the kitchen table for days. I hated to see them go. (The great thing about plasticine, of course—compared with the kind of clay I had as a kid—is that it doesn't dry out, so you can use it over and over again.)

## Paper Shoes?

 Another idea from the Henry family. Leah, age seven:

I trace around my feet on either thin white paper or colored construction paper and cut it out to make the sole. Then I put a strap over the top for a sandal, or I make harder designs, like loafers and saddle shoes. Tape holds the pieces together. I decorate them with crayons, magic markers or stickers. I've made shoes for everyone in our family and for our dolls, too.

## Collages . . . and More

  Anna and Justine have enjoyed "collage" making—cutting pictures out of magazines and pasting them on big sheets of cardboard. The fun part is coming up with dramatic, bizarre or funny juxtapositions.

I secretly like it because I think cutting up advertisements and putting them back together again with a new "logic" encourages the kids to think about how advertisers project images to create an effect on us.

Anna has lately begun turning her collages into "magazines," each with a name and its own theme, featuring particular types of pictures.

## BUT WHAT CAN I DRAW OR PAINT?

### Become an Illustrator

"A child who loves to draw might like to do what I did," Lindsay Mugglestone told us:

I illustrated my favorite books. It's a great challenge to get down on paper what you see in your mind's eye. You don't have to show them to anyone if you don't want to. But they're sure to absorb much time, energy and imagination. If my pictures turned out good enough, I taped them into the book.

### Cartoon Capers

My good friend Gretta's seven-year-old son, Casey, loves to draw cartoon strips with a story, then make a drawing of a TV set with slits on both sides. "He pulls the story along as if it were on TV, but he's in control," says Gretta.

Cartoonist Leonard Rifas creates a cartoon version of Add-On-Stories (page 25) with his friends. They each do a panel and pass it on. Even if you're not a cartoonist, this can be fun.

### Balloon-Print Murals

Another suggestion from Debbie Coyle's pre-school involves "painting" with balloons. It's a regular favorite with her children and their parents.

First mix the paint: 2 parts liquid starch to 1

part dry tempera works well. (Rainbow colors are great; blue and green make an "ocean.")

Blow up balloons (sturdy ones) to a size a child can grasp. Some bigger ones for adults. Then roll out a long expanse of paper—white shelf paper or newsprint roll ends.

Dip the balloons in the paint and then let everyone bounce the balloons up and down on the paper until all the white is covered. If you use rainbow colors, a beautiful effect can be achieved by having people move from left to right, somewhat overlapping the colors.

Once a year, our kids create an "ocean" with blue and green paint. Then they cut out paper fish to stick on the paint while it is still wet.

## Dribble-Squish

Another favorite of Debbie's preschoolers uses the same paint mixture as Balloon-Print Murals.

Apply the paint to prefolded pieces of paper with droppers. (You knew those vitamin droppers would come in handy for something!) Dribble the paint down the fold or on one side. Then fold and squish! The paper opens to reveal mirror images. (If you don't have droppers, dribble from straws.)

## Patio-Door Picasso

Those of you who have big glass doors or windows—have you ever imagined they could become canvases for your budding Picassos? Claire Wickens tells how she even came out with clean windows to boot:

First we mixed up the poster paints from easily stored powders, located our largest brushes and got the children enclosed in smocks—except on hot days, when old shorts would do. We picked out the boundaries. Then they went to it.

Erasing was easy, with a damp rag. A low stool helped the shortest child make full use of his area. Sometimes we left the pictures for a few days; sometimes a photo was in order. And cleanup was just as much fun (I often picked a painting day when the windows needed washing anyway). Soapy water in buckets, long-handled squeegees and especially the garden hose with a nozzle was a delightful way to spend a hot afternoon. As for clean windows, I'll admit there was a bit of finish work for me, but not much.

### Decorating the Big Outdoors

The Mullins family in Cordova, Alaska, have a novel idea for brightening their yard:

We decorate a big salmonberry bush outside our kitchen window. Sometimes we put red "pretend" apples on it and green and purple grapes. At Thanksgiving, polystyrene "popcorn"; at Christmas, lights and ornaments. During snowy times, we hang icicles and shiny-colored glass balls on it, which catch the lights. (I keep looking for these items at rummage sales.) At Easter, we blow one-hundred or so eggs, put strings in them, color them, and hang them on the tree—our "eggplant!"

These decorations brighten up our often-dull days.

### Eye-nomatopoeia

One workday not so long ago, Anna was out of school, and I was working in my study. She wanted to be near me. And I enjoyed her presence. So she came up with a quiet activity that didn't distract me *too* much.

She asked me to say a word, any word, and she would write out the letters in a way that captured the spirit of the word. *Cold* might be dripping with icicles or covered with snow. She made the letters in *Fight* with boxing gloves on, actually fighting each other. We've included some to give you the idea.

### Taking Advantage of Special Events

Suzanne Williams reminded us that special events are good for getting kids involved in special projects.

Our local library recently had a design-a-bookmark contest for kids. Katie actually wasn't old enough to fit the age categories, but I cut a bunch of paper for her and let her use colored markers. She stayed busy and enthusiastic for several hours at a time, two days in a row, while I worked in the other room. She didn't win any prizes, but one of her creations was displayed with a ribbon on it, and she was pleased by the whole thing.

## Putting on Your Own Art Show

 After viewing a very "whimsical and involving" art show at a local gallery, Suzanne Copeland's boys and friends from down the street (ages six to nine) put on their own art show:

They spent a feverish afternoon nailing, gluing and assembling and painting wood scraps and doing easel painting as well. They created a gallery full of art in just a couple of hours. I asked if they would like to show their work, and they snapped up the idea. Soon they had cleared and swept our front porch and installed the show, complete with professional information cards showing their name, year of birth, name of the piece, media and collection.

They invited some other neighbors to view it. They were so proud. We kept it up for a week.

## Artists' Club

 When Lisa Van Dusen was about ten or eleven, her friends started their own artists' club called Natura Felici. It's Italian for "happy nature."

Our club converted a loft in our barn into an artists' studio. We thought of ourselves as the Michigan version of the Paris Left Bank. We even made our own little gallery in the barn where we could hang all of our paintings. And we had showings to which we'd invite our parents and friends.

We began this chapter with tips for making art easy for kids—an ordinary part of enjoying life—and ended with kids inventing their

own ways to make their artistic creations into *extra*ordinary productions. We hope that parents reading our book will conclude not that they *owe it to their kids* to make art more accessible but that it could be just plain fun for them, too.

## Resources for Bringing Art into Your Family Life

Bos, Bev. *Don't Move the Muffin Tins.* Roseville, Calif.: Turn the Page Press, 1982. "Full of child-centered art projects," says Debbie Coyle.

Brashears, Deya. *Art Experiences for the Very Young.* 1 Corte Del Rey, Orinda, Calif. 94563. More than one hundred art ideas—spiral bound and color coded according to medium use. "These are art ideas, not crafts," the author told me. "I mean that they involve a lot of creativity, and no two kids' products will come out looking alike. I've taught art for 12 years, and these are my kids' favorite projects. They can be adapted to two-year-olds and up to any age." Also recommended by Debbie Coyle.

Frank, Majorie. *I Can Paint a Rainbow.* Incentive Publications, 2400 Crestmoor Dr., Nashville, Tenn. 37205, 1976. Recommended by Karen Goodkin, the children's first art teacher, who inspired their artful spontaneity.

Silberstein-Storfer, Muriel, with Mablen Jones. *Doing Art Together*. New York: Simon and Schuster, 1983. Molly Sullivan likes this book because it has a lot of information about setting up a workspace in your home.

*Syd Hoffman Shows You How to Draw Cartoons*. New York: Scholastic Book Services, 1979. Includes interesting pictures drawn in four simple steps. "At age four, Katie enjoyed tracing the completed pictures," Suzanne Williams told us, "and at age five she likes using the book as it was intended."

Wiseman, Ann. *Making Things: A Handbook for Creative Discovery*. Boston: Little, Brown, 1973. In two volumes, these books look good because the ideas don't require a lot of special materials. The illustrations are simple and clear.

Withers, Andrew. *How to Make Cards for All Occasions*. New York: Crescent Books, Crown Publishers, 1972. Another Suzanne Williams recommendation: "A beautiful, colorful book with a variety of intriguing designs that should give a nudge to the creativity of anyone, child or adult. Even a preschooler gets inspiration and ideas from it." (Not in print, but try the library.)

# 7
# Writing for Pleasure

**B**ecause much of my livelihood comes from writing—and my study is right in the middle of our house—writing is a commonplace activity around here. Since the line between my "work" and my leisure is blurry at best, I think I convey to my children that writing *can* give great satisfaction—even if they have suffered through some of my panic deadlines.

Anna and Anthony were very fortunate when they were younger to have attended the San Francisco School, which stressed creative writing. When Anthony was in the third and fourth grades, he was asked to write a one- or two-page dramatic story almost every evening. These challenges let his sense of humor come through.

## DIARIES THAT AREN'T "DUTIES"

 I remember as a teenager trying to keep a diary—one of those with five lines for each day and a little gold lock to keep your brother out. Generally, I just recorded what some boy I had a crush on did or said to me that day. I don't recall it being very satisfying.

I like my daughter's approach much better. She doesn't feel she has to make an entry every day. Her book is one of those lovely cloth-covered ones so commonplace now. (There are no lines with dates to make you feel guilty if you leave one blank.) In Anna's words:

I write in my diary whenever there's something

really important I want to remember. When I
can, I put photos in to illustrate a particularly
special time. I put in pictures of my friends at a
party we had at my house last year when we all
dressed up in really formal clothes. I like to
draw borders around the pictures to make them
look even prettier.

## CLUBS AND NEWSLETTERS . . . OR REAL-WORLD JOURNALISM

Creating special clubs, with special meeting places, is one
of my most fun memories of childhood. When I was Anna's age, my family lived on an island in the middle of
the Pacific Ocean—Wake Island. We had no TV, of
course. Except for short-wave, the only radio was WAKE, the island
station on which both my mom and brother (at age twelve) were disc
jockeys—in other words, our "canned" entertainment was pretty
primitive.

But as the island was only nine miles long, with no more than one
hundred moving vehicles and fewer than one thousand inhabitants,
our parents could let us roam freely, without worrying. As long as
we knew how to swim well, there was little harm that could befall
us. So, our clubhouses were more exotic than most. One was simply
in a little clearing in a really dense thicket near the lagoon. Another
was a Japanese dugout remaining from World War II.

There were only two people in my special club. But our limited
membership didn't matter. We had a special name, the SBL Club,
the meaning of which we swore never to divulge in our entire lives.
And I never have.

Our club even had a special language that no one else could understand. We simply spelled every word backward. So, *gum* became
*mug* and I became *Secnarf*. Each week we had vocabulary lists to
memorize. We progressed in our "language study" to the point that
we could converse fluently enough at the dinner table to stump our
parents and brothers. Of course, that was the whole point!

Anna's club, the Pythons, has regular weekly meetings just like we did, only they are a bit more sophisticated. The Pythons have a weekly club newsletter. Members rotate responsibility for writing and photocopying it. It's only for members, so I can't tell you all its features. But one week it had a crossword puzzle. A regular feature is the "quote of the week."

## Children's Express

 But did you ever imagine that kids could be real reporters? Why not?

Since 1976, Children's Express has given thousands of kids the opportunity to participate in real-world journalism. With thirteen the maximum age of reporters, it's a news service *by* children but *for* everyone. When just getting started, its reporters scooped more than five thousand adult journalists to get the two biggest stories of the 1976 Democratic Convention. Now Children's Express stories are carried over the UPI wire service—that means they are carried in thousands of papers throughout the country.

Why not see if there's a bureau of Children's Express near you? They're in New York City; Salem, Massachusetts; Newark, New Jersey; Alameda, California; as well as three overseas. (The address of the main office: 20 Charles Street, New York, New York 10014.)

We enjoyed this insight of Gilbert Giles about why Children's Express has been so successful: "My main advantage," said Giles, twelve, "is that adults don't think children listen or understand."

## WRITING FOR FUN

### Letter-Writing Adventures

  Both Anna and Anthony have enjoyed having pen pals. Even if the relationships don't last long, the thrill of receiving a letter from a distant, mysterious friend is terrific.

Suzanne Williams suggests that we can encourage our children, even very young ones, to write letters or illustrate ours:

> Family members love to get letters from kids, with or without translation, and writing them can keep a child out of your hair for at least a few minutes while you do your letter writing.

When kids love a particular book, why not encourage them to write the author? (As a writer, I know how special this can be for us, too.) Alan Gussow (remember the Sunday morning house cleanup, page 47?) recalls his son, Adam's, letter to a favorite author:

> Adam's very first book he read all by himself was *James and the Giant Peach*. He wrote a letter to Roald Dahl and a month or so later received a wonderful hand-written letter from Dahl from Great Missendon, England. Adam was thrilled. He wrote to William Pène du Bois after reading *The Alligator Case*. Not every author will write back—at least there is no certainty, but I would suggest that children be encouraged to try. We have friends our own age who as children wrote to authors and got back many, many letters.

Remember the Severens in chapter six—sewing and weaving? Well, they also developed a letter-writing tradition that lasted many years:

> After Sunday breakfast, we'd all write one or two letters to family or friends. The children loved it. As soon as they began writing, letters would return in the mail. Anna is still a faithful and constant writer.

## Kids Writing "Books"

When Anna was in the fourth grade, her teacher, Marian Vaughn, came up with a super idea to encourage the kids to write. Each child in the class wrote a short story, which was improved by the suggestions and editing of other children. These stories were compiled into a book, which Marian had photocopied with a colored cover and simple binding.

Then we had a book-publication party! All the children and parents were invited to our house for a potluck. The books were distributed, with the name of each author called out and the title of their story recognized. Parents paid enough for them to cover the copying costs.

That book will be a lifelong treasure. I thoroughly enjoyed all the stories—not just my daughter's.

You might want to plant the seed of such an idea with your children's teachers.

## Making Books—At Any Age

*. . . From Toddlers*

Even very young children enjoy the whole idea of putting together a book of their creation. Suzanne Williams gives us this example of her daughter's fun:

> At four, Katie was attracted to a Christmas stencil book we'd bought at a half-price sale. I helped her pop out the stencils. Then she delighted in tracing the shapes onto scratch paper and writing a line or two on each page, telling a story about the bells, stars, Santa and all. Then I stapled the pages of her book together in the order she requested.

Another suggestion for young children comes from Betty Henry. Why not ask your three- or four-year-old to dictate a story to you?

You can write it out—one line to a page. Then the child can illustrate her or his very own tale.

Older children can have fun making books for their younger siblings, especially alphabet books. Each page can have one word or one sentence—or even a poem for each letter. Then the younger child can make the illustrations.

"Shape books," where all the pages are cut in the shape of the book's subject, are another fun possibility.

### . . . To Adults

Remember the game Geography that opened our book? My brother, Gil, who invented it is far and away the funniest member of our family. At one point we were all pushing him to become a stand-up comedian, but he decided to become a mathematics teacher instead. And how can we feel bad? Wouldn't it be wonderful if there were more math-teacher comedians?

Anyway, Gil also illustrates the fact that anyone can write for pleasure . . . and occasionally even profit. A couple of years ago a light bulb clicked in his crazy head—why not write and publish a "California Passport"? It would look as much as possible like a real one but be full of jokes about California. There's certainly no dearth of material there!

And he did. The passport to the "Free State of California," blue with an embossed gold seal, has been ordered from as far away as the Middle East. To give you the flavor, imagine an official-looking page for personal information including:

> Birthdate (or Sign)_____
> Occupation_____
> But I'd Rather Be_____

But perhaps the "Facts about California" and the "Declaration of Oath" are the funniest parts. The oath concludes,

> I swear that, as a Californian, I will not act in a
> smug or superior manner, even though I have

every reason to do so. I further swear that
although I may not agree with another person's
opinion, I will defend to the death his right to
put it on a T-shirt. I pledge and swear that if I
build my house in a canyon, near a fault line or
on the side of a hill, and if it should then burn,
crumble or slide onto the house below, I will
not be greatly surprised. Finally, I solemnly
swear that I will deal sternly with those who
advocate the return of the work ethic and in
extreme cases will suspend their hot-tub
privileges.

My brother and my parents have marketed it by taking it to gift
shops and bookstores and by inexpensive ads in local magazines.
Although it has never been a best-seller, what began as a crazy idea
has helped put my brother through school. (If you'd like to be among
the privileged holders of a California Passport, just write to Gil at
JGM Productions, 4226 Folsom, San Francisco, Calif. 94110.)

## And If You Don't Like It . . . Rewrite It!

 "Unhappy about how a book has been writ-
ten?" asks Suzanne Copeland. Well, you can
take charge. I like this idea:

Discuss the problem(s) and rewrite the book
with your children. If the book is from the
library, of course you can't change it physically.
If it's a book you own, you can actually cut and
paste with sticky labels to improve any manner
of problems—attitude, language, method of
dealing with problems, grammar, punctuation
and so on.

## Poems . . . Serious or Silly

 Since my writing is all nonfiction, I've been particularly in awe of my children and their friends' poetry. Their interest in writing poetry started with special teachers who gave them the confidence to get started. Anna's class went to the local art museum, and each child wrote a poem based on her or his reaction to a favorite sculpture, painting or display. Toward the end of the year, the class put on a special poetry reading for parents and friends.

Encouraged to write poetry in school, Anthony and Anna have gone ahead and written poetry at home on their own. For all you kids reading this book, we want to include three of Anna's first poems, written when she was eight. They show that poems don't have to be serious or soupy.

### Alone

*Sitting alone on the beach*
*is like having a feast on chicken bones*
*or a five-story dollhouse*
*which has nothing in it but air.*

### Forgive

*I forgive you for everything you did to me, EXCEPT*

*for smashing a lemon meringue pie into my face,*
*and wiping a spoon that just came out of a bowl of chile right across*
*my face,*
*and putting a frog down my shirt,*
*and making me close my eyes and walk into the boys' bathroom,*
*and making me go to the store in a bathrobe,*
*and telling me it wasn't cold out so I wore shorts and a tube top and*
*it turned out to be 5 below zero,*

*Oops! That's everything you ever did to me!*

## Rescue

*Have you ever rescued someone? I have.*
*Once a girl was about to jump off a building when I saved her by*
*shouting: Don't jump!*

*What a rescue!*

*Another time a kid who just learned how to swim tried swimming*
*to the dock and I yelled after him: You won't make it!*

*What a rescue!*

We bought Anna a binder where she can safely preserve all her
poems.

But some families have taken poetry into a whole other realm.
Margo Nanny's family is one of them:

> Now that we're grown, we rarely turn on TV
> when the family's together. Our latest pastime
> has become writing poems about family events
> and family secrets. They're usually funny, and
> Dad's now taping them and making a collection,
> and I'm putting them on my computer. Dad's
> even starting to write them, which is such fun,
> since he can't spell, and so we have new ways to
> tease him.
>
> Generally, when we think of new material for
> a poem, my sister and I go into the back room
> with a bottle of wine and spend an hour
> laughing about how we're really gonna "get"
> Dad now. When we emerge with something, the
> family gathers around, Dad gets out his tape
> recorder and we start some kind of ridiculous
> performance, which we usually end up
> performing at the next several family gatherings,
> until someone slips up and gives us new
> material, at which time we get out the bottle of
> wine, go into the back room and start it all over
> again.

One poem my sister and I wrote when our
dad went on a business trip. When we picked
him up at the airport, he had friends with him
and we sang it in the airport bar, after a few too
many Irish coffees!

If you doubt that you're as clever as the Nanny family, don't be
discouraged. You could still have just as much fun, no matter how
silly your inventions. Remember, no one's judging!

# 8
# Music in Our Lives

Opening our chapter on art in our everyday lives, I stressed how unartistic I am, to convince you that you don't have to be "talented" to bring the pleasure of art into your home. Well, if my artistic talent is minimal, my musical talent is zilch. (My brother used to put his hands over his ears when I tried to sing as a child. I thought he was being cruel, just trying to hurt my feelings. Later, I found out it was self-protection!) Nevertheless, both my kids are enjoying developing their musical abilities—Anna on the piano and Anthony on the guitar. Their basic sense of self-confidence was established in the music program of the San Francisco School, where their teacher, Doug Goodkin, made music something all the kids could enjoy. I'll include some of his tips in this chapter.

## INTRODUCING MUSIC TO YOUNG CHILDREN

 Let's begin with ideas for introducing music into the lives of very young children. Here's a suggestion from Suzanne Williams:

> When Katie was three, we saw the need for
> either a children's record player and records or
> some substitute. We decided on a cassette tape
> player that plays through our hi-fi.
> Katie immediately learned our rules of

operating the player (it was okay to use Stop,
Play and Eject but not Fast Forward or Rewind)
and never abused them. When we had extra
space on a tape after recording a story, we'd fill
it up sometimes with something of our
choosing, such as classical music, just to give
Katie more exposure to it.

Later, when preparing for a train trip to
Colorado, we also bought a portable cassette
player that kept Katie well entertained. We also
used it during a long car trip.

Very important is discovering ways to allow young children to
enjoy whatever musical instruments you have. Suzanne and Katie
have some ideas here, too:

As soon as I saw that Katie understood the
color coding on the music that came with her
toy xylophone, I made a color-coding chart for
one octave of our piano and began writing songs
for her in a little looseleaf notebook with a
bright cover.

She delighted in playing the piano virtually
every day for a period of about a year. A new
song (her choice of several) was often her
reward for being a good girl when we went
shopping or whatever. Her book grew to about
forty or so songs, including many Christmas
carols. Some even had two-finger chords, which
she begged for and felt very good about
learning.

When she got tired of the piano and just
wanted some "pretend" music she could sing to,
we bought a very cheap used guitar. A musical
friend told us that it couldn't be tuned in any
regular way, so she tuned the strings to play a D
chord. That way Katie can strum a melodious
chord that she's convinced goes beautifully with

all her favorite songs, such as "Angels We Have
Heard on High" and "Oh Come, All Ye
Faithful."

Suzanne also came up with an ingenious way of introducing Katie
to music with special meaning:

> Part of our routine each Friday is to call the
> church office and find out which hymns will be
> sung on Sunday. Then we can look them up in
> the hymnal we have at home, sing them or play
> them, or talk about what the words mean.

### Learning to Listen

Doug, Anthony and Anna's first music teacher, told us
how his experience in Asia changed his expectations
about what young children can appreciate:

> In Asia we saw that from a very early age
> children heard the music, saw the dance, learned
> the stories through the drama that were their
> cultural heritage. So we've made it a practice to
> take our daughter to the music and dance
> concerts we go to since her infancy; now at four,
> she's a perfect audience member.

## GAMES WITH MUSIC

### Clap 'n' Play

At the San Francisco School, clapping games were among
Doug and the kids' favorites. Says Doug,

For centuries, children's games have been the vehicle for children's musical expression. I see no reason why parents can't join in the fun! Partners clap their own and each other's hands in a set pattern to a song. "Pat-a-Cake" and "Say-Say-Oh-Playmate" are two familiar examples.

Drawing from your own childhood and your child's playground experience, you're bound to discover many such plays that you can use spontaneously in those moments of hanging around—waiting for the bus, after dinner and so on. When they get boring, change one thing for variety, that is, do it in slow motion, as fast as you can, with three people instead of two or make up your own clapping pattern.

## Tap-a-Tune

 Anna's fifth-grade class has a special relationship with people living at Chapparal House, a nearby home for the elderly. They have visited often. In sharing memories of her own childhood, one of the women from Chapparal offered this idea:

At the dinner table in my family, I would tap out the beat of a song. My brother would try to guess the song. Or vice versa. The winner, naming the song, got the other's dessert!

## Pass the Rhythm

 Mark Gordon suggests a musical version of the old game of Telephone, or what we used to call Gossip. Using rhythm sticks, or any tapping objects you have around, let one per-

son invent a simple rhythm pattern. The idea is to pass the rhythm down the line without changing it, or to make changes—like speeding it up.

## Name That Tune

 If someone in your family is musically gifted, here's a game we've had great fun with. It's our version of the old TV show "Name That Tune." Peter plays the opening bars, and Anna and Anthony try to be the first to guess. Of course, you could play the same game with records or tapes.

## Why Not BE the Music!

 Doug and his four-year-old daughter, Kerala, have a lot of fun with the piano, too—and you don't have to know how to play to try this idea:

> With my daughter, I'll play things that suggest movements without worrying about what notes I play. When I play slowly using low notes, she walks around heavy and plodding, like an elephant or a monster. With high, fast notes, she's on her tiptoes, perhaps a bird. I play fast up and down, and she runs—when I stop, she freezes as quickly as she can. I can play marching, skipping or swinging rhythms, and she responds accordingly. Then we switch, and she plays while I dance. If we want to make the sounds "prettier," we just use the black notes on the piano.
> So many home have pianos that just become furniture, little realizing what an endless source of creative expression and family communication a piano can be without a single piano lesson!

## MAKING MUSIC

 Sometimes my kids ask me to listen to their practicing. I try to see those moments as special for me, too—as moments when I can sit down, catch my breath and give them my full attention. I am not able to offer advice or help. But knowing I am really listening no doubt motivates them to try harder.

I've been impressed that from almost the beginning of her instruction, Anna's piano teacher, Andrea Simms, has encouraged her to write her own music—something I thought only prodigies could do! But, no, all her students are composers. (Anna particularly loves to play her own compositions.)

If you, a parent, play a musical instrument yourself, you can do much more. Matthew Gaines, age ten, tells what it feels like to play with his dad:

> I'd been playing guitar for only about two
> months. But the improvement was amazing. I
> like playing with my dad more than playing
> alone. For one thing, I may learn something like
> a new chord, or maybe even teach my dad a
> new song, like "Billie Jean." I know my dad
> likes playing with me because he likes to see my
> progress.

But to make music, you don't need a piano, a guitar or a flute. Anthony and Anna learned in Doug's classes that one can make music with almost any object. Gwen Greene, with a one- and a three-year-old, captures the spirit:

> We sing a lot, all the time, but particularly
> holiday songs at holiday time. We do a lot of
> drumming with wooden spoons on the tables or
> on coffee cans with plastic tops. We clap to
> music and beat the table, or any flat surface,
> with our hands.

## Spontaneous Songs

 Both Anthony and Anna have enjoyed making up their own songs. Doug told us about how he encourages his own four-year-old, Kerala, in spontaneous singing:

> For over a year now, Kerala has spent hours on end singing songs she's made up as she goes along. On our walks together, whenever she complains that "her legs hurt" or starts asking, "When are we going to get there?" on a long car ride, we ask her if she'll sing a song. She'll start singing about whatever she sees—the telephone poles outside the window, the flowers we walk by, one image flowing into the next. These epic songs can go on for as long as an hour!
>
> Sometimes she'll repeat parts over and over again until they solidify into an identifiable song, at which point we'll ask her to teach it to us and record it on cassette tape.

Doug's experience reminds us of the perspective of folksinger Pete Seeger: "One shouldn't think of a song having to be permanent. If you make up a song and it's only good for one afternoon or one evening of singing, that's fine. Is a souffle any less great for only lasting a few minutes?" (From *A Song Is a Rainbow* by Patty Zeitlin. See page 157.)

To encourage singing, Sally and Gordon Lake keep their twins' records and player in the kitchen and play them "before, during and after meals":

> After they have sung a particular song for months (dozens and dozens of times), we sometimes make up joke versions, which the kids adore: "Wreck the halls with boughs of

ivy"; "Sailing, sailing, over the bounding drain";
"The pear went over the mountain."

## Rituals in Song

 Songs to begin the day, song-prayers to pre-
face our meals, songs at bedtime to relax and
comfort—these are rituals that fortify our
lives. In the Henry family one lullaby everyone loves goes like this:

> *Go to sleep now my darling*
> *You must tuck in your toes*
> *If you sleep well my darling*
> *You will turn into a rose*

New verses are created by changing the words *toes* and *rose*, which
don't make much sense anyway! "So we tuck in our elbows and turn
into a cauliflower or tuck in our tummy and turn into a refrigerator,"
says Betty. "The variations are endless."

Amelia Ross-Gilson, age fourteen, loves being awakened every
morning by her mother's "Good Morning Song":

> *Good Morning, Amelia*
> *You've slept the whole night through.*
> *Good morning.*
> *Good morning*
> *To you.*

Clearly the possibilities of enjoying music with our children are un-
limited. The only obstacle is often our own self-consciousness, which
fades as we discover the pleasure for ourselves.

## Resources to Bring More Music into Your Home

Coyle, Debbie. *Did You Ever Sing a Mooley Cow?* Dee Wanger Publications, 2113 Creekwood Drive, Fort Collins, Colo. 80525, 1984. A collection of one hundred traditional children's songs, including simple autoharp (easy-to-learn string instrument) instructions and a cassette tape with the melody for all one hundred songs. Great for the nonmusician! And for children who want to learn a simple instrument.

Jones, Bessie, and Bess Lomax Hawes. *Step It Down: Games, Plays, Songs and Stories from the Afro-American Heritage.* New York: Harper and Row, 1972. Recommended by Doug Goodkin. (It's not in print, but try the library. It's worth it, says Doug.)

Kenney, Maureen. *Circle Around the Zero: Plays, Chants and Singing Games of City Children.* Magnamusic-Baton, 10370 Page Industrial Blvd., Saint Louis, Mo. 63132, 1975. Also recommended by Doug Goodkin for its fun music games.

Musician Nancy Shimmel, the daughter of musician and songwriter Malvina Reynolds, laments that it is hard to find good children's records in most stores. She recommends the following sources, which do mail order and will send you a list of what they have to offer:

> Children's Book and Music Center
> 2500 Santa Monica Boulevard
> Santa Monica, Calif. 90404

> A Gentle Wind
> Box 3103
> Albany, N.Y. 12203

She recommends her mother's *There's Music in the Air: Songs for the Middle-Young* and *Tweedles and Foodles for Young Noodles*, both records available from Schroder Music Company, 1450 Tenth Street, Berkeley, Calif. 94710.

Her favorite book for introducing music to children is: Patty Zeitlin. *A Song Is a Rainbow: Music, Movement and Rhythm Instruments in the Nursery School and Kindergarten.* Glenview, Ill.: Scotts-Foresman, 1982. Written for teachers, it has good ideas for parents, too, plus an excellent list of records and books.

# 9

# Just Plain Fun

While many of the activities in this book can be done by children either on their own *or* with adults, here we want to talk exsively about the crazy, fun things kids do by themselves when not plopped in front of the TV.

Mulling over the ideas we wanted to put in this chapter, it suddenly hit me that maybe one of the reasons parents allow their children to watch so much television is that, while viewing may be withering or warping their minds, at least their bodies are immobilized. Mom and Dad don't have to wonder whether their child is falling out of a tree or crashing a bike into the neighbor's fence or doing any of the other antics that kids do manage to do. (Hmm, maybe one could make the case that television has reduced the number of broken young arms and legs.)

In any case, some of the activities that follow are pretty boisterous. We can assure you, however, that there have been no broken limbs in our family.

### Pillow Possibilities

 Pillows seem to offer limitless possibilities for kids. Why not pick up extra pillows at garage sales or second-hand? I combined some old pillows by making big, colorful slipcovers for them. They stayed in the play area with the toys. Kids can use pillows to mark out a playhouse floor plan. Or, they can become imaginary stepping stones over a dangerous, rushing river, or cars in a train going anywhere. And pillow fights are fun for kids of any age.

## Sock Slide

 A young friend of ours has another idea that you can try if you have either a linoleum or a smooth hardwood floor:

We used to slide across the linoleum floor in our socks. We marked how far each of us could slide and even kept records.

## In-Door Dangling

 We have a chinning bar in the doorway connecting my study and the hall. The chinning bar went up several years ago with the thought that it would be good for gaining upper body strength and also good, as we were told, for the back—just hanging helps lengthen a tight back.

Well, the kids have been the chief users, and not in the ways I had imagined.

Anna and her friend Nikki (who is an accomplished gymnast) discovered that the chinning bar could become a mini-gym. Standing on the kitchen stool, they take turns leaping for the bar and swinging back and forth. (Needless to say, I don't get much studying done during this activity.) Anna was thrilled when she finally grew tall enough that she could jump and clasp the bar without help from a chair or a lift.

During the 1984 Summer Olympics Anna's fun on the chinning bar was recharged. After watching the feats of the Olympic medalists, she developed special turns in the air and concentrated on her form and coordination. "I ended up getting blisters," she said. "But I borrowed Anthony's baseball gloves, and that helped." (Be certain, of course, that the chinning bar is securely installed. We nailed wooden blocks under ours to give it extra support.)

## Playroom Action

 Our house in San Francisco had a very big, funky basement piled with junk. A good cleanup and a few coats of sky-blue paint transformed the place into a cheerful playroom.

We put up a colorful—huge—hammock that a friend brought us from Mexico. The kids spent hours with their friends using it for a nice reading spot, but, more often, swinging each other. It would hold two or three kids at a time.

We also put up a plastic mock-tire swing. The great thrill there, of course, is winding oneself up as tightly as possible and then spinning until you can't walk straight. And when Anna was still on a tricycle, we made an obstacle course that she would have to steer her way through.

Suzanne Copeland adds these suggestions for the playroom: a chaise-lounge pad on the floor for tumbling, a rope ladder for climbing and 2-by-4-foot balance beam on the floor. In adding any new play equipment, I'd suggest that you watch your kids closely the first few times they use it. You can see whether they are old enough to use it safely.

## Snow Play

 Snow play offers endless possibilities. One I had never thought of before comes from Betty Henry:

> Kids love making and solving mazes. Tramping
> them out in deep, fresh snow is fun; marching
> them out of damp sand at the beach is just
> about as good.

It's not surprising that from Alaska I received some novel ideas for ways kids enjoy leisure time without TV. From fisherwoman Sheelagh Mullins, a mother of four in Cordova, Alaska:

> A big success here is when we paint the snow
> once or twice a year. I use powder paints and
> also food colors. We fill plastic liquid soap
> bottles and spray the snow. It's a neighborhood
> event.

You might want to make sure the kids restrict their creativity to their own yards.

## Chalk Mazes

 If you don't live in snow country, Linda Ream's five- and eight-year-old sons have an alternative "maze" idea. Says Linda,

> The boys have fun drawing huge mazes with chalk on the driveway that people play on similar to Hopscotch. I've even noticed the garbage man going through it!

## Kids' Garage Carnival

  "Putting on a summer carnival in our garage served both as a social event for the whole neighborhood and a stimulant to the imagination and power to organize," says Claire Wickens:

> All the children got into the act (I had very little to do with it except some low-key supervision and food preparation).
>
> The carnival often came after a thorough cleaning of the game closet and rooms. We always had a stack of small gadgets, trinkets, unwanted small items like those fuzzy rings, plastic magnifying glasses and the like. These served as prizes. As they say, one man's junk is another man's treasure—and our carnivals proved it.
>
> The carnival required a great deal of planning—setting up the games, preparing the food, making the signs to advertise around the

neighborhood and also the tickets plus cleaning out the garage.

Many of the games were typical carnival replicas:

- Throwing Ping-Pong balls into cans (not bottles on the cement floor) filled with water, all at varying distances; coffee cans are ideal
- Throwing bean bags (they had to be sewn the first year) into buckets or through a hole in an old sheet
- Fishing over a cardboard wall and receiving one of those trinkets on the other end of the line
- Shooting a dart gun with rubber tips onto a target
- Bowling balls toward a stack of empty tin cans
- Magician games; in one, you place a bean under one of three cups, switch them around quickly and let others guess which cup hides the bean

We also used games from our game closet that were appropriate.

Each "customer" bought tickets for a penny; each game cost one or two tickets. The object was not to make money. But the money added adventure. The kids also sold food—popcorn, orange juice or lemonade, cookies—and one year we pulled out some outgrown books to sell for five cents each..

Some of our ideas did not work out—the superballs bounced down the street! But, needless to say, the neighborhood kids loved our carnivals as much as our children loved staging them.

## The Virtues of Empty Space

Just as "empty" time can open up possibilities, so can empty space. So many of the activities in this chapter take *room*. Lisa Van Dusen points out that empty space—that hallway or unfurnished room that adults might rush to fill up—is in and of itself a great instigator of fun: "We used to dance and dance and do acrobatics in our nearly empty front hallway. That empty space inspired great activity."

Lisa's comment reminded us that for a period of about a year when the kids were tiny we lived in a very big house in New York. On our budget, we couldn't think of properly furnishing it. While I regretted its vacant look, the kids loved it—riding tricycles from dining room to living room with no obstacles in the way. Maybe when our kids are little, we should resist the urge to fill up the empty spaces.

## Working in the Real World

In chapter three we talked about Anna's volunteer work at my institute. Are there similar possibilities in your neighborhood? A couple of ideas from Suzanne Copeland:

At our recycling center, young helpers unload our trunkful of newspapers and bottles and help by ripping apart recycled telephone books and by doing odd jobs to assist the older workers.

When I was about eleven and twelve, I "worked" at the city swimming pool each summer morning, as a helper in the Red Cross swimming program. In exchange for my helping teach youngsters to get their faces wet and to float, I got a free swimming pass for the season and a feeling of being very grown up.

Remember that *every* chapter in our book includes many activities that kids have come up with on their own. So, kids, please don't overlook the possibilities.

## Other Suggestions for Kids' Play

These books are no longer in print, but they are worth looking for in the library:

Allison, Linda. *The Sierra Club Summer Book.* New York: Sierra Club Books/ Charles Scribner's Sons, 1977. Lots of neat ideas for summer, from how to make a "gum-wrapper thermometer" to the fun of a slippery slide using the water sprinkler. Plus games.

Milberg, Alan. *Street Games.* New York: McGraw Hill, 1976. A big book full of happy pictures. Everything from Capture the Flag to Flipping Cards to five different varieties of Hopscotch from different cultures. Just skimming through this book could keep my kids engrossed for hours.

# 10

# Home as a Place to Learn about the World

Through our family lives, we form enduring perceptions of the world around us and other people. Are they threatening images instilling fear we will later have to conquer? Are they condescending images of backwardness? Or are they positive images of the diversity, depth and dignity of other cultures?

We're not suggesting that we turn our homes into geography classrooms, but rather that we give some thought to the way we bring the world into our homes, into the lives of our children.

## LEARNING ABOUT THE WORLD

### Radio News

 At dinnertime throughout America many families huddle around the TV, watching the evening news. Unfortunately, this means bringing nightly the horror of war, crime and disaster right into our homes. Sure, children must learn what is going on in the world. But I believe that the unremitting focus on the most negative, and often demented, aspects of our world can rob children of hope. They have little context in which to place all the bad news.

We've discovered radio news to be a significantly different experience. First, you don't see all the frightening images. In general, radio news is less sensational—maybe because it can't use pictures to shock us. Second, the radio doesn't "take over" quite the way TV

166

does, so it seems easier to get into a conversation about what you are hearing. Talking about the news is most important. You want your children to know which of the events mean something to you, and to them, and why.

Often we have National Public Radio's "All Things Considered" or the local listener-sponsored KPFA news on in the evening as we are preparing dinner. When the kids were younger, they used to sit around the kitchen table drawing or doing their homework while the news was on.

Anthony was eight in 1979, when the revolutionary war in Nicaragua reached its climax. The TV news carried pictures showing the horror of Somoza's bombing of civilians. On radio, we heard about it. But, without the pictures, it didn't leave us totally devastated ourselves. We could therefore talk about *why* people were fighting— how the majority of Nicaraguans had been deprived of land and even enough food to eat.

This is just one example, of course, but I remember it because the information stuck: This spring Anthony chose to write a paper about Nicaragua.

### Magazines, Books, Maps—All within Reach

Even very young children will be attracted by vivid pictures of different cultures, leading to many questions about how other people live. We need only keep the resources out and available so that our kids can pick them up and go through them at their own pace. For her preschooler, Suzanne Williams keeps "a good selection of attractive, inexpensive reference books that we've bought used (so we've had no qualms about putting them out for Katie)."

Like many parents I've talked to, Suzanne has discoverd that some books aimed at adults are equally intriguing to kids—books, for example, highlighting a geographic region, or special historical attractions, large atlases or paperbacks describing flowers, birds and trees. "Katie has spent hours examining these books, asking questions, telling us what she's seen and what she'd like to see," Suzanne tells us.

Museum stores are good sources of such materials.

One pictoral reference book that Anthony has enjoyed is the *National Geographic Picture Atlas of Our Fifty States* (Washington, D.C.: National Geographic Society, 1978). The *Children's World Atlas* (Millbrae, Calif.: Celestial Arts, 1981) also looks good.

Betty Henry's family keeps a world map pinned to the dining room wall. It's especially handy when the news is on. "I remember the Falkland Islands crisis," Betty told us. "The kids wanted to know where the Falklands were. When they found them on the map and discovered they were so far from England, we had to explain some history. I think we all learned something!"

Fred Mindlin has put a special map—a relief map of his home state, California—up in his living room. (Most kids, like my kids, are fascinated by relief maps.) Fred's daughter also loves to plot their car trips.

Globes are handy, too, and can be acquired secondhand. Our friend Sheila Wilensky-Lanford, who owns the OZ bookstore for kids in Southwest Harbor, Maine, told us that now there's even a stuffed globe on the market—"Hugg-a-Planet"—for young children. Any big toy store is likely to carry it.

The most important advice in all of these suggestions, however, is to keep these resources available—not tucked away in the study— but right where your family spends most of its time, and where you sit or listen or watch the news.

### There's More Than One Way to Look at Something

The Institute for Food and Development Policy, which I helped to found, has recently published the Food First Curriculum to help grade-school children understand the roots of world hunger. We've been pleased that teachers find that the curriculum activities don't leave children despairing and hopeless. Just the opposite, they tell us: Children feel empowered because they are dealing with real problems. (You can order it from the Institute for Food and Development Policy, 1885 Mission Street, San Francisco, Calif. 94103.) Many of the activities in the curriculum could easily be adapted to home time.

One of the purposes of the Food First Curriculum is to help children learn to read and listen critically—to understand that even stories that are presented as "fact" have a point of view. One activity you might try at home:

> Pick one news story and have different family members follow its coverage on various media— TV, radio, papers, magazines, especially if you have access to those of opposing political persuasions. Ask friends how they see it. Then talk about the differences. Try to figure out *why* there are differences.

## HOW DO OTHER PEOPLE LIVE . . . AND THINK?

### Foods from Faraway

 Dinnertime is an opportunity to learn about the world in yet another way—through what we eat.

Why not try focusing on one part of the world for, say, a week? You might bring into your home picture books on that part of the world or get some photos out of an old *National Geographic* to put up on the kitchen wall. Then, during the week, you could experiment with dishes from that part of the world.

For example, Middle Eastern dishes are fun for kids because they include finger food. Here's a simple recipe from *Diet for a Small Planet*. It's a filling for pita (pocket) bread.

For a special humous, blend in a blender until creamy:

> *2–3 cups cooked garbanzo beans*
> *½ cup toasted ground sesame seeds OR*
> *¼ cup sesame butter*
> *2 cloves garlic, crushed or minced*

*2 tbsp lemon juice*
*¾ tsp ground coriander*
*½ tsp ground cumin*
*cayenne pepper and salt to taste*

(If the kids don't like the spices, you can cut them out
and the flavor is still good.) Fill a pita bread pocket with
this blend, along with shredded lettuce, tomatoes, cu-
cumbers, onion and so on. A dollop of yogurt on top
makes it all even better.

On their nights to cook for the whole family, Anna (ten) and Alexander (twelve) Severens prefer to use the Children's UNICEF cook-
book. (Terry Touff Cooper and Marilyn Ratner, *Many Friends Cooking*, U.S. Committee for UNICEF, 331 East 38th Street, New York,
N.Y. 10016, 1974.)

### Where Does Our Food Come From?

 To answer that question, the Food First Curriculum suggests that it might be fun to search the cupboards and
make a list of all the imported foods. The next step might
be to find the countries where the food originated on a
map or globe.

Or, at dinner, ask your children to try to identify which foods have
come from another country. A conversation might follow about what
we know about the lives of people who produce our food.

### Games from Faraway

 Another window into other cultures is the
games people play. I remember when Anna
learned Chinese jump rope, for example. It
seemed like much more fun than our own
standard version. We uncovered a book that can lead your family
into lots of fun from other cultures: *The Second Cooperative Sports and
Games Book* by Terry Orlick (New York: Pantheon, 1982).

Just one example: In New Guinea groups of kids gather in the shallow water to play Wol Wol. Everyone stretches out their arms to the side and spins themselves around. When a signal is given, everyone must stop instantly. The challenge is not to fall into the water! Origins of other games in this book range from the Canadian Arctic to the Australian outback.

## The Language Window

 But perhaps the best window into other cultures is language. We can encourage our children to begin early in mastering a second language—by demonstrating how satisfying it can be ourselves. I've been studying Spanish for several years, and now that Anthony is in his second year of Spanish at school, we enjoy practicing together. Last year, Anna's fifth grade put on "Goldilocks and the Three Bears" in Spanish. It was delightful.

To stimulate interest in a foreign language with young children, you might want to get *My Everyday French Wordbook* (also for Spanish; Woodbury, N.Y.: Barrons, 1982). It tells about everyday activities. The illustrations are great.

## Music and Art from Faraway

  Tom Zink reminded us that most libraries lend records as well as books. His has a good collection of folk songs from around the world:

> You can bring home Swiss yodelers, Irish balladeers and Africa drum bands for free! Following that could be learning about the dances those people do with the music, or making up your own original dance.

Karen Goodkin suggests that we can learn about other cultures through art projects, too. She recommends *Art from Many Lands* by

Jo Miles Schuman (New York: Prentice-Hall, 1981). The multicultural art projects "can be done now in this country by kids with our resources," says Karen.

## IT'S A WORLD WE CAN CHANGE!

In our homes either we learn to perceive the world as alien and overpowering, in which individual efforts account for little, or we come to view the world as changing everyday in response to the initiatives of millions of people—a world inviting us to contribute to positive change by living according to our deepest values.

The trick for parents is to make clear our own values and to engage our children in the challenges of the real world without loading them down with guilt and fear. What a delicate task!

We each have our own style. I myself try not to preach or coerce. I don't, for example, try to dictate what my children eat outside of our home. My goal is to set an example, not a dogma that my children will have to rebel against later. For those of us whose life work is social change, I think this is especially important.

Perhaps most important is simply to include our children in discussions of social problems and our responsibilities. One of my favorite memories of my own childhood was my parents' impromptu gatherings of their friends. Sitting around the kitchen table drinking coffee, they gabbed a mile a minute about the political and social issues of the day. I wouldn't always listen, or grasp it all when I did, but what stuck was the feeling that being grown up meant grappling with important and exciting ideas.

### Joining in Social Action

We can also invite our children to participate in any civic action that we take. Even going to the polling place on Election Day can be a big thrill for a young child.

I've invited, but never demanded, the kids to go with me on demonstrations for causes I believe in. Sometimes they've come, sometimes not. Last year, for example, Anna and I spent an afternoon together putting flyers for candidates we supported in the mailboxes of voters on the day before the election. This year she went with me to Ohio and Michigan to investigate the working and living conditions of farmworkers.

## Directing Our Dollars

 Another excellent idea from *Peacemaking* (see full citation on page 179) is to involve the whole family in deciding which social change organizations to support out of family income.

Why not make this an annual discussion? You could collect all of the direct-mail fundraising appeals and other descriptions of programs you might want to consider. Then let the whole family discuss the possibilities, including both the aims and potential effectiveness of the various approaches.

You might want to talk together about what portion of the family income you want to give away. I am eager to try this suggestion, for it would seem to be an excellent way to bring our values to the surface and to consider our responsibilities to the needs of others.

## Books for Change

 Books about people making a difference in this world can leave enduring impressions of hope. For older children, there are many biographies of people who have left a mark in history. Here we've included only a small sample of inspiring stories of people children may never have heard of, some quite "ordinary" people—both real and fictional—who have made a difference:

Ruth Franchere, *Cesar Chavez* (New York: Thomas Y. Crowell, 1973). Helps us understand the plight of farmworkers through the life of one man.

Ruth S. Meyers and Beryle Banfield, editors, *Embers: Stories for a Changing World* (New York: Council on Interracial Books, 1983). One of my favorites in this rich collection is the story of Rosa Parks, who by refusing to give up her seat on a bus to a white man helped launch the civil rights movement.

Institute for Food and Development Policy, *Food First Comic* (1885 Mission Street, San Francisco, Calif. 94103). Written with humor, this is a story of a teenager who sets out to determine for herself whether world hunger is inevitable because of food scarcity. She overcomes the skepticism of a boyfriend and her teacher and learns what she can do to make a difference.

New Mexico People and Energy Collective, *Red Ribbons for Emma* (New Seed Press, Box 3016, Stanford, Calif. 94305). Tells of the courage of a poor Navaho woman who stands up to the coal and power companies in order to protect her ancestral land.

Barbara Smucker, *Runaway to Freedom: A Story of the Underground Railway* (New York: Harper and Row, 1977). This is one of Anna's favorites.

But we don't want to discriminate against the famous! The Bobbs-Merrill Company (New York and Indianapolis) has a "Famous Americans Series" for children ages seven to ten. Anna and her friend Justine especially like the biography of Susan B. Anthony by Helen Albee Monsell.

I have included these books because they can inspire kids to see the significance of individual action, even when faced with overwhelming odds. But many children's hope for the future is blighted by fear about nuclear war. How can we talk compassionately and intelligently about a subject that terrifies us, too? Here are two thoughtful resources:

Kate Cloud et al. *Watermelons Not War! A Support Book for Parenting in the Nuclear Age* (New Society Publishers, 4722 Baltimore Avenue, Philadelphia, Pa. 19143).

William Van Ornum and Mary Wicker Van Ornum, *Talking to Children about Nuclear War* (New York: Continuum, 1984).

## Celebrating Our Differences

In contrast to TV's frightening images, we can choose to bring books into our homes that build curiosity about those different from us, empathy for those whose lives are more difficult, and respect for those who demonstrate courage and positive leadership. And these don't have to be books we push on our children. Many of Anthony and Anna's favorite books are in this category.

Here are only a smattering of possibilities, many especially recommended by our friend Shiela of the OZ bookstore and by Anna:

Verna Aardema, *Bringing Rain to Kapiti Plain* (New York: The Dial Press, 1981). (Ages 4–8.) Vibrant illustrations with a rhyming story that really shows life in an Africa village. "The plot was fun," says Anna.

Kathleen Rice Bowers, *At This Very Minute* (Boston: Little, Brown, 1983). (Ages 4–8.) At bedtime, a young girl is wondering what goes on in other parts of the world. Somewhere hurt feelings are mended, a tractor is fixed. But farther away, it is already tomorrow, it may be winter, a child may go to bed hungry. This clever story idea could stimulate parents to make up their own variations.

Eleanor Coerr, *Sadako and the Thousand Paper Cranes* (New York: Dell, 1977). (Ages 8–12.) A moving story of a young girl who dies of leukemia ten years after living through the bombing of Hiroshima. Anna *loved* it.

Muriel Feelings, *Jambo Means Hello: Swahili Alphabet Book* (New York: The Dial Press, 1974). (Ages 4–8.) A different view of learning about letters.

Jean Fritz, *Homesick: My Own Story* (New York: Dell, 1982). (Ages 8–14.) The author's own life, ages ten to fifteen in China (until 1927), is depicted with special warmth and poignancy. Anna's review: "It kept you on the edge of your seat. I really started to care for Jean."

Huynh Quang Nhuong, *The Land I Lost: Adventures of a Boy in Vietnam* (New York: Harper and Row, 1982). (Ages 8–14.) A glimpse of daily life in Vietnam before the destruction of war. "This is a great book for kids my age [ten]," says Anna. "It's exciting, interesting and true!"

Tillie S. Pine and Joseph Levine, *The Chinese Knew* and *The Africans Knew* (New York: McGraw-Hill, 1958 and 1967). (Ages 6–12.) Part of a series of books highlighting discoveries from many cultures. Learn how to make the inventions yourself—from lampblack ink to an abacus. (Out of print, so please try the library.)

Norma Simon, *Why Am I Different?* (Chicago: Albert Whitman, 1976). (Ages 4–8.) Even includes a child who feels different because his parents don't want a TV!

Peter Spier, *People* (Garden City, N.Y.: Doubleday, 1980). (All ages.) In a class by itself, full of delightfully detailed drawings that celebrate human diversity—physical, cultural, religious . . . everything. It was recommended to us by Shiela's daughter, six-year-old Brook Wilensky-Lanford, who loves the "different languages." Her parents report that she will spend hours studying and tracing the dozens of language scripts Spier includes. Although beginning readers could enjoy *People*, even Anthony at thirteen found it captivating, and so did I.

Mary Beth Sullivan, Alan J. Brightman and Joseph Blatt, *Feeling Free* (Reading, Mass.: Addison-Wesley, 1979). (Ages 9 and up.) "It made me understand that people with disabilities are just like me," commented Anna.

## Opening to the Many Cultures That Are America

*The Family of Man* (New York: Simon & Schuster, 1955), *The Family of Women* and *The Family of Children* (New York: Grosset and Dunlap, 1979 & 1977). (All ages.) My kids have been intrigued by these three classics. (They include nudity, so you need to decide whether you feel they are appropriate for your family.)

Scott O'Dell, *Sing Down Moon* (New York: Dell, 1970). (Ages 8–12.) The life of a fourteen-year old Navaho girl. We experience her people's forced migration from their original homeland in Arizona to Fort Sumner, New Mexico.

Louisa R. Shotwell, *Roosevelt Grady* (New York: Dell, 1963). (Ages 8–12.) Life as a migrant worker seen through the eyes of a young boy who wants to live in one place long enough to stop being an outsider and to learn.

Elizabeth George Speare, *Sign of the Beaver* (New York: Dell, 1983). (Ages 8–12.) The story of a thirteen-year-old white boy and the incredible friendship he develops with an Indian boy.

Joshiko Uchida, *Journey to Topaz: A Story of the Japanese-American Evacuation* (New York: Charles Scribner's Sons, 1971). (Ages 8–12.) Fiction based on fact, this tells of Japanese families uprooted and confined in camps during World War II.

## GIVING MODERN-DAY MEANING TO HOLIDAY RITUALS

 Holidays offer us an opportunity to learn about the world and ourselves. But it takes a little effort to cut through the commercialized, packaged versions of our holidays in order to help our kids and ourselves uncover the age-old values that can renew our lives. One quite helpful guide to developing more meaningful, less materialistic holiday rituals is the *Alternatives Celebrations Catalogue* (P.O. Box 429, Ellenwood, Ga. 30049, 1978).

Rhea Irvine, our skilled helper in writing this book, attended a Seder at the home of good friends of hers—Kathy Kolman and Clyde Leland. The Seder, or Jewish Passover, commemorates the exodus of the Jews from Egypt, or the beginning of Jewish independence. Passover refers to God's "passing over" the homes of the Jews when he sent plagues to convince the Egyptian pharoah to let them go. The Seder is the traditional meal held on the first and second nights of the week-long celebration.

Clyde explains the genesis of their very special evening:

> Every year it seemed like the kids weren't understanding the meaning of the Seder story. So I tried to write our own Seder that could tell the story as history and relate it to the issue of freedom in a way the kids could grasp. I think I succeeded. A couple of months after the Seder, our family was driving home from a weekend trip when Ramona (age four) asked us to tell the Passover story again. So we did, and then we ended up talking about the underground railroad and about Harriet Tubbman (a leader in the underground railroad, helping blacks escape slavery), who is in our Seder story.
>
> And I told the kids, "You know, there's an underground railroad now—people trying to get out of El Salvador. People help them cross the borders into Guatemala, Mexico, and the United

States. They even dig tunnels. They get here
and are hidden by people.

Our seven-year-old Jacob asked: "Are they
slaves?" We explained, "No, but they are afraid
of being jailed or killed."

Kathy and I were really surprised at how the
Seder did seem to help them better understand
what is happening to people today.

Kathy came up with another innovation for the Seder. Concerned
that the children might get restless during the rather lengthy evening,
she taped butcher paper to the tables and put out coffee cans of felt
pens: "Drawing together did turn out to be an easy way for people
to meet," Kathy told us. "One table drew animals around each plate."

Clyde would be happy to send anyone interested a copy of the
Seder he prepared. Just send $3.50 for copying and postage to Clyde
Leland, Box 3479, Berkeley, Calif. 94703.

Five years ago Colleen and Milo Shannon-Thornberry decided to
break with their usual family Christmas. They decided to spend
Christmas Eve at their church's shelter for the homeless:

For the week before Christmas the dining room
table was covered with socks and goodies being
wrapped for the shelter's thirty "guests." As we
loaded presents into the car for the trip to the
church, visions of Christmases long ago came to
mind. At the shelter, carols, remembrances
shared, lots to eat and *joy* filled our evening and
Christmas morning.

It was about 10:30 when we left for home on
Christmas morning. On the way home,
Katherine, then eight, piped up, "This was the
best Christmas ever. It's the first time I didn't
feel greedy." Like Katherine, we all learned a lot
about the spirit of Christmas that year.

## A FINAL THOUGHT

In my early twenties I was one of those troubled young people who
didn't want to have children because the future of the world looked

too bleak. Unless I myself had hope, having children seemed like a cruel imposition on them.

But by my late twenties my life began to come into focus. Hope grew in me as I began to see what I might contribute. From my experience with Anthony and Anna, I've concluded that the most important ingredient in giving our children hope is what we choose to do with our own lives. If children see their parents participating, working with friends and neighbors toward a better life for us all, they will have hope. In other words, while all the great resources mentioned in this chapter are important, more important are the decisions our children see us make every day. Do we ourselves act out of hope or retreat out of fear?

And the beauty of it is that we get back from our children redoubled whatever positive attitudes we project to them. They become the source of our joy. For remember, kids are born with boundless hope—our job is just to make sure it is allowed to live.


## Other Resources

Good general resources for all the concerns raised in this chapter include the following:

Haessly, Jacqueline. *Peacemaking: Family Activities for Justice and Peace*. New York: Paulist Press, 1980.

McGinnis, Kathleen and James. *Parenting for Peace and Justice*. Maryknoll, N.Y.: Orbis Press, 1983.

# ⚡ 11 ⚡
# TV—But
# We're in Control!

**W**hen Anthony was about five and Anna was just turning three, I decided that it was much easier just to get rid of my TV than to agonize over how much was "too much" and which shows weren't "too bad." We didn't have a TV at all for almost eight years. I never had a moment's regret. But since not many of you will want to adopt my drastic cure, the challenge becomes: How can we take control of TV instead of letting it control us?

I've been consistently struck by how many people refer to their relationship to TV as an addiction. "It's like a drug!" I've heard umpteen times. (And I was convinced that the television industry had come to the same realization when billboards went up in our neighborhood reading, Get Your Daily Dose of "Dallas.")

Marc Gunther, columnist for the *Hartford Courant*, sums the problem up nicely:

> Most Americans don't watch programs. We watch television. One network executive called it the "LOP" theory of viewing. He said that most people plop themselves down in front of the tube without even knowing what's on, and then seek out the LOP—the Least Objectionable Program.

Here are some clues for relieving this addiction for ourselves and our families:

180

## PUTTING TV IN ITS PLACE
### Scheduling

My good friend Gretta Goldenman has a workable arrangement with her seven-year-old son, Casey. At the beginning of the week, Casey sits down and selects exactly which shows he wants to see that week. The TV goes on for those shows only. This way, Casey thinks about his choices, and he and Gretta can talk about them. Of course, parents can simply set down an hour(s)-per-day limit. But Gretta's approach encourages more critical thinking.

Or how about limiting TV watching to certain days only? I favor this approach over the so-many-hours-a-day strategy because your family can then get used to the novelty of a totally TV-free environment. It takes some time for new traditions to develop in a family. If an evening is cut up by even an hour of TV, it's less likely that other activities will emerge.

Other friends are experimenting with the new gadgets that block out certain channels or certain times. The point is to arrive at an arrangement that minimizes the potential for repeated conflict about TV watching.

Eventually, as I said earlier, we did get a TV. (For how can we write about what to do when you turn it off, if we don't have one to turn off? we joked.) But ours sits in the closet until there is something special we want to watch. Which is pretty rare. Since it takes some effort to haul it out of the closet, we aren't apt to do it idly, just to see what's on.

I recall talking with a radio interviewer recently who told me that his kids will just flick on the set whenever they pass by. "It's just habit." Keeping the TV out of sight, and making it somewhat inconvenient to turn on, is the simplest way to fight the LOP syndrome.

### Creative Viewing

 Another approach to putting ourselves in charge is to become creative viewers—or at least reactive rather than passive viewers. On one level, that simply means talking over the programs and commercials, analyzing with our kids the implicit messages we're getting.

Some have come up with clever devices to keep their families alert to the destructive messages. Betty Henry uses the following "score-keeping" device:

> I don't like TV, but my children love it. To make it acceptable, I sometimes prepare headings on a large piece of paper, such as Mean Things People Do and Nice Things People Do, Girls Doing Interesting Things, Boys Doing Interesting Things, Healthy Foods or Junk Foods. My daughter makes checks under the heading each time it is appropriate. Sometimes we compare PBS to network TV.

Jerry Mander, author of *Four Arguments for the Elimination of Television*, whom you met in chapter one, uses another score-keeping device to explain the impact of TV. Jerry travels around the country talking to kids, but you might want to try his idea at home with your family. Here's his account of one such presentation to school kids in Rae, a small town in Canada:

> After turning on the TV, I asked the children to count the "technical events." I explained that a technical event is an alteration of the image on the screen by technical means, a change in an image that couldn't possibly happen in ordinary life. For example, a sudden cut from one face to another face, or to another room. A camera switch, so that you are now behind some action that an instant ago you may have been above. Suddenly you are outside, or in a car, when an instant ago you were in a room. The viewer moves forward or backward in time. Cartoon images appear. Objects dance. All of these interventions are introduced for the purpose of heightening viewer interest.
>
> An average commercial television program has about ten technical events per minute. In

advertising, however, especially the expensively produced prime-time national advertising, there are likely to be twenty to twenty-five technical events per minute, sometimes more.

I asked the class to join me in counting technical events aloud. They did so with enthusiasm. It was fun, actually, and my hope was that during that evening, at home, with the TV on, these kids would find themselves continuing to count the technical events. Perhaps it would cause a degree of distance from the immersion.

You might want to try counting with your kids, comparing commercials and programs.

One of our reviewers asked, so what's so bad about technical events? It's not that technical events are bad in themselves. The point is that these manipulations keep our attention held so tightly that we don't stop to ask, Do I really want to be watching this anyway? So Jerry's counting suggestion is simply intended to put us back in charge.

## Audience Participation

 We think of TV as totally passive. We just sit and stare. Yet, music and dance programs invite us to join in, if we just let go of our inhibitions. Remember Margo Nanny's delightful family poems? Here is another recollection from her childhood:

One of my greatest childhood memories was our weekly family viewing of Lawrence Welk. We couldn't wait to watch it because we'd always dance to the music and stand on Dad's feet as he waltzed us around, and we'd giggle and laugh as Mom and Dad danced. We also learned songs from the show, which Mom would later play by ear and we'd all sing.

## COMMUNITY IN ACTION—"FARMINGTON TURNS OFF!"

In chapter one, I described Farmington, Connecticut's "TV Turn Off." In January 1984, 1,047 people in Farmington did what many thought was impossible: They went cold turkey. They turned their TVs off for the entire month.

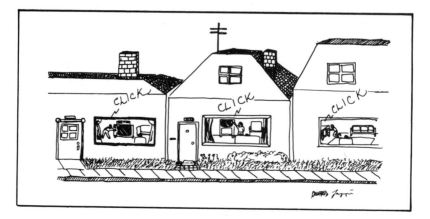

It all began when the town librarian, Nancy DeSalvo, cooked up the idea of a town-wide "TV Turn Off." Evidently she "hit a nerve," as Mrs. DeSalvo puts it, for within months she had not only the Library Council but the Town Council and the Board of Education behind the scheme. "Be it resolved that because excessive television viewing detracts from the educational growth of children and the quality of family life," they all said, we urge, "all Farmington residents to eliminate or drastically reduce television viewing during the month of January, 1984."

To add extra incentive, the library passed out "cold turkey" pledge cards and special "Farmington Turns Off!" bumper stickers for those brave souls willing to survive a month without TV. The library also promised special activities during that month and sponsored an essay contest entitled "What I Did When I Turned Off the TV." A local merchant offered prizes for the winning essayists—one thousand books, of course!

Participation was impressive. Mrs. DeSalvo estimates that 75 percent of preschoolers participated, and almost 60 percent of junior high school students. Not everyone went cold turkey, but at least their viewing was significantly reduced. Overall, she estimates that in a town of six thousand households, more than one thousand families completely stopped watching television, and at least a quarter of the population was affected.

But what neither Mrs. DeSalvo nor anyone else anticipated was the media attention that swept down on their little town. "Overnight," joked the superintendent of schools, "our office became a booking agent for the media." *USA Today* carried a front-page story; the *Today Show* interviewed several of the participants; media from as faraway as Ireland and Australia rang up. Mrs. DeSalvo estimates that the library gave four hundred interviews! They had hit a nerve, indeed.

I visited Farmington, a well-heeled suburban hamlet on the outskirts of Hartford, just two months after the "TV Turn Off." I was curious about what had motivated the people who had instigated it. And I wanted to know more about the impact of this attention-catching scheme.

Middle-aged and the mother of six, Nancy DeSalvo struck me as a dignified, devoted librarian, not a social crusader. Yet she, clearly, was the force that had made it all happen. With the early spring afternoon sun pouring into the big windows of her spanking-new library, Mrs. DeSalvo piled stack after stack of the evidence—clippings, essays and questionnaires—before me.

Of course many parents and teachers worry about the insidious effects of TV, and many researchers have gotten Ph.D's. documenting the problem. But what makes Nancy DeSalvo different is that she decided to *do* something. We all know what she proved—that sometimes it only takes one committed person to make big things happen.

My hunch as to why Farmington's "TV Turn Off" "clicked" is that it gave people community support for what many had wanted to do for so long. In chapter one we told of Sandy Goralnick's experience with her three-year-old daughter, whom she feared was a real "addict." Yet, by mid-January, Jenny had kicked the habit:

If I had tried to do this alone, if I had said no myself, I would have gotten so much flack. I would have heard a lot of whining, trying to change my mind. But with the group aspect, with the whole town involved, it was set—fixed. So my kids just accepted it.

In reading the essays the kids wrote and talking to teenagers who work in the library, it was obvious that January had been a month of discoveries. The first was that it wasn't too hard after all. "When I think about 'no-TV,' it gets hard, but then if I forget about it and get on with things, it's simple," wrote eighth-grader Arlene Gavalis in her essay. She joined friends at school playing basketball, even though "I'm quite a klutz. . . . While other people go home and watch soap operas from three to four, we are having fun and getting exercise." She goes on to tell of reading more, too.

Here are some other observations from the "cold turkey" kids:

· Seventh-grader John Johnson: "I went down to the cellar a lot to scrounge around. I found a bunch of old broken crayons and learned to make candles by melting them down. I also found an old gun scope and took it apart to get the prism."
· "I drew pictures for my family and made several get-well cards for my aunt. . . . I would do my homework without rushing," wrote third-grader Mary-Grace Vendola. (A number of the kids said their grades went up in January.)
· "When my teacher said, 'Well, who's going to turn off their TV?' moans filled the air," wrote eighth-grader Christy Kelly. But deciding that she "watched TV too much," Christy did turn off. "Now I take walks, do puzzles and latch-hook rugs for fun. . . . I hope I can continue to use my leisure time so well."
· "I got extra sleep on weekend mornings because I didn't get up early to watch cartoons. I learned how to make carrot curls while my mom was making dinner. I made a bird feeder," second-grader Jeff Goralnick wrote. "I earned extra money by doing chores around the house."

· "I finally got enough time to clean that messy room of mine," sixth-grader Darcy Lynn Wollenberg wrote. "That took two and a half hours."

· "The most favorite thing I did was that I talked and listened to my family. Boy, did we have fun!" said Brendon Blair.

· And Brian Kelly, a sixth-grader, contributed what he called the "true confession of a TV addict":

> I'm the guy you read about in the statistics on TV viewing. I could watch TV all day and then all night. I could always find something to watch. My mother thought she was raising three children and a turnip (that's me).
>
> Then came "cold turkey," and the TV was silent and blank. The first few days I was in a state of shock—my body moved, but something was unusual with my mind. My "mini-screen eyes" were focusing on games, puzzles, books and so on. My ears were listening to new sounds, like the sound of my sled runners crunching through the snow. My senses were returning . . . . Here it is the end of January and the end of "cold turkey." I had a few weak moments, but I made it!!!!
>
> Will someone please tell me: Did the Fall Guy fall? Has the A Team become the B Team? Has General Hospital become a private hospital? Have Tom and Jerry signed a truce? Or maybe, Has Brian conquered his addiction to TV? is the important question. I hope so because I don't want to be a turnip.

Janice Newton, the kindergarten teacher you met in chapter one, made a discovery, too. Although she reported that she couldn't discern big differences in individual children, she did notice a big difference in her class as a whole. "The children were less tired, their play was less violent and they were better listeners. The children talked more about many activities they had participated in with their families. Many more books were brought in for us to read because they were 'good books Mom or Dad had read.'"

In Farmington's "TV Turn Off" many participants felt they had definitely gained. Susan Blair really put her finger on it when she observed that the greatest benefit was

> the *pride* we all gained in being committed, of surviving (and enjoying!) "doing without," of stretching ourselves in the pursuit of something new (and I guess somewhat daring!). Like any other discipline that we endeavor to follow, if we are successful (and we were in many ways!), we grow, we learn about ourselves, we take pleasure in the fact that we have done so well.

Three teenagers who work after school in the Farmington library submitted the following entry to the essay contest. We think it is a fitting conclusion for our book.

### The TV Turnoff

by Becky Wheeler, Margo Wollenberg and Tim LeBouthillier

We believe this whole idea was hatched in Nancy's head,
On a boring day last summer when the library was dead.
We all said she was crazy when she told us of her plan.
Could she really be successful with a full scale TV ban?

After listening to her motives we agreed to play the game.
Yet little did we know we were on our road to fame.
For one whole month we'd turn it off to prove that we could
    do it.
For some it would be easy, yet others would not live through
    it.

We enjoyed a warm response from the adults of the town,
but when it came to kids our age they really laughed us down.
When January finally came we kissed our set good-bye.
We pulled the plugs, and packed them up, and then sat down
    to cry.

What would we do without the box that gave us so much fun?
It sustained us, entertained us, and to us was number one.

Soon our sadness was forgotten when the press arrived in town.
We grew more and more excited as our names were written
down.

Soon the TV shows we watched were thought of less and less.
The small campaign we started had earned national success.
Without TV our lives did change, for the better we must say,
We were keeping ourselves busy now with every passing day.

We now had time for homework, playing games and having fun,
causing trouble, spending money, we were always on the run.
But now the month is over and the ban has now been lifted.
Yet somehow deep inside we feel our TV views have shifted.

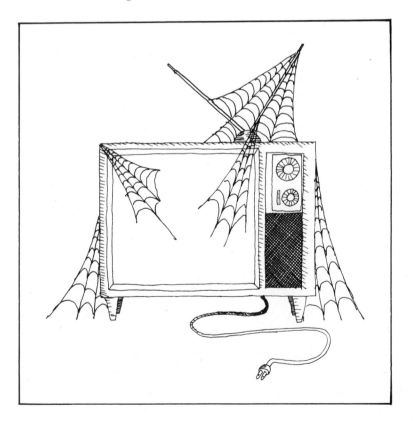

We learned more things that fateful month that we may not
admit.
There is a world outside TV, all we must do is find it.
So cheers to Mrs. DeSalvo, and all who helped us see,
that there are many more things to do in life than sit and watch
TV.


## Other Resources

Due to the tremendous interest generated by its TV Turn Off, the Farmington Library has put together a kit to help other towns, libraries or
schools that are considering a similar project. Anyone interested in pur-
chasing the kit—with a planning guide, a publicity plan, sample press re-
leases and more—should write for further information to Nancy DeSalvo,
Farmington Library, 6 Monteith Drive, P.O. Box 407, Farmington, Conn.
06032.

Nancy DeSalvo has also compiled the following selected bibliography:

For parents and professionals:

Bryant, Jennings, and David Anderson. *Understanding TV: Research in Children's Attention and Comprehension.* New York: Academic Press, 1983.

Honig, Alice Sterling. "Television and Young Children," *Young Children,*
May 1983.

Kaye, Evelyn. *The A.C.T. Guide to Children's Television: How to Treat TV
with TLC.* Boston: Beacon Press, 1979.

Liebert, Robert M. *The Early Window: Effects of Television on Children and
Youth.* 2nd ed. New York: Pergamon Press, 1982.

Medrich, Elliott A. *The Serious Business of Growing Up.* Berkeley: University
of California Press, 1983.

Piers, Maria. *The Gift of Play.* New York: Walker and Co., 1980.

Singer, Dorothy G. and Jerome L., and Diana M. Zuckerman. *Teaching
Television: How to Use TV to Your Child's Advantage.* New York: The Dial
Press, 1981.

Trelease, Jim. *The Read-Aloud Handbook*. New York: Penguin Books, 1982.

Wilkins, Joan Anderson. *Breaking the TV Habit*. New York: Charles Scribner's, 1982.

Winn, Marie. *Children Without Childhood*. New York: Pantheon, 1983.

For children:

Angell, Judie. *First the Good News*. New York: Putnam, 1984.

Berenstain, Stan and Jan. *The Berenstain Bears and Too Much TV*. New York: Random House, 1984.

Bond, Michael. *Paddington on Screen*. Boston: Houghton Mifflin, 1982.

Brown, Marc, and Laurene Krasney Brown. *The Bionic Bunny Show*. Boston: Little, Brown, 1984.

Cohen, Miriam. *Jim Meets the Thing*. New York: Greenwillow, 1981.

Heide, Florence P. *The Problem with Pulcifer*. New York: Harper and Row, 1982.

McPhail, David. *Fix-It*. New York: E. P. Dutton, 1984.

Phelan, Terry Wolfe. *The Week Mom Unplugged the TV*. New York: New American Library, 1979.

# Activity Index

The following is a complete alphabetical listing of the activities described in this book. Beside the name of each activity you will find a symbol (or two or three) that corresponds to the coding used in the book to help you determine which activities are appropriate for your family. A circle (●) indicates which are good for the whole family, a triangle (▲) which are suited for kids by themselves, and a square (■) which are best for the very young.

# About the Author

FRANCES MOORE LAPPÉ is best known for her classic bestseller, *Diet for a Small Planet*. First published in 1971 by Ballantine Books, *Diet for a Small Planet* has now sold almost three million copies. Ms. Lappé is the author of many other books, including *Food First: Beyond the Myth of Scarcity* (Ballantine Books, 1979), which she co-authored with Joseph Collins. With Collins, she co-founded the San Francisco-based Institute for Food Development Policy, a not-for-profit public education and documentation center with twenty thousand members. As a leading spokesperson for the growing number of individuals and organizations concerned about world hunger, she has received many awards and honorary doctoral degrees.

Frances Lappé is the mother of two children, Anthony and Anna. She knows well the joy of leisure time creatively spent with her family.

# About the Author

FRANCES MOORE LAPPÉ is best known for her classic bestseller, *Diet for a Small Planet*. First published in 1971 by Ballantine Books, *Diet for a Small Planet* has now sold almost three million copies. Ms. Lappé is the author of many other books, including *Food First: Beyond the Myth of Scarcity* (Ballantine Books, 1979), which she co-authored with Joseph Collins. With Collins, she co-founded the San Francisco-based Institute for Food Development Policy, a not-for-profit public education and documentation center with twenty thousand members. As a leading spokesperson for the growing number of individuals and organizations concerned about world hunger, she has received many awards and honorary doctoral degrees.

Frances Lappé is the mother of two children, Anthony and Anna. She knows well the joy of leisure time creatively spent with her family.